50 Valentine Lunch Recipes for Home

By: Kelly Johnson

Table of Contents

- Heart-Shaped Grilled Cheese Sandwiches
- Roasted Red Pepper and Tomato Soup
- Strawberry Spinach Salad with Poppy Seed Dressing
- Love-Infused Chicken Caesar Wraps
- Creamy Avocado and Tuna Salad
- Sweetheart Caprese Salad
- Spicy Shrimp Tacos with Cilantro Lime Slaw
- Heart-Shaped Pizza Pockets
- Mediterranean Quinoa Salad
- Roasted Beet and Goat Cheese Salad
- Heart-Shaped Beet and Hummus Sandwiches
- Chicken and Strawberry Salad with Balsamic Vinaigrette
- Smoked Salmon and Cream Cheese Crostini
- Spinach and Feta Stuffed Chicken Breasts
- Mini Heart-Shaped Quiches
- Lobster and Avocado Toast
- Pesto and Sun-Dried Tomato Panini
- Creamy Tomato Basil Pasta
- Heart-Shaped Turkey and Swiss Sliders
- Greek Chicken Gyros
- Roasted Veggie and Hummus Wraps
- Strawberry and Goat Cheese Bruschetta
- Heart-Shaped Ravioli with Alfredo Sauce
- Bacon-Wrapped Stuffed Mushrooms
- Caprese Stuffed Avocados
- Spicy Chicken and Avocado Salad
- Sweet and Sour Meatball Skewers
- Herb-Crusted Salmon with Lemon Dill Sauce
- Heart-Shaped Tomato and Basil Pesto Puffs
- Honey Mustard Chicken and Apple Sandwiches
- Heart-Shaped Sweet Potato Fries
- Shrimp Scampi Linguine
- Warm Spinach and Artichoke Dip
- Grilled Veggie and Pesto Flatbread
- Creamy Butternut Squash Soup
- Heart-Shaped Pancetta and Egg Breakfast Sandwiches

- Pear and Blue Cheese Salad
- Heart-Shaped Cornbread Muffins
- Spaghetti with Garlic and Olive Oil
- Balsamic Glazed Brussels Sprouts
- Roasted Red Pepper and Spinach Frittata
- Spicy Tuna Stuffed Avocados
- Heart-Shaped Savory Scones
- Chicken and Waffle Sliders
- Thai Peanut Chicken Salad
- Mini Heart-Shaped Calzones
- BBQ Chicken and Pineapple Wraps
- Sweet Potato and Black Bean Tacos
- Creamy Mushroom and Spinach Orzo
- Heart-Shaped Sweetheart Sushi Rolls

Heart-Shaped Grilled Cheese Sandwiches

Ingredients:

- 4 slices of bread (your choice, such as sourdough, whole wheat, or white)
- 2 tablespoons unsalted butter, softened
- 1 cup shredded cheese (cheddar, mozzarella, or your favorite cheese)
- Optional: 1 tablespoon mayonnaise (for added creaminess)
- Optional: Additional fillings like tomato slices, ham, or bacon

Instructions:

1. **Prepare the Bread:**
    - Using a heart-shaped cookie cutter, cut out heart shapes from the bread slices. Depending on the size of your cookie cutter, you may be able to get two hearts from each slice of bread.
2. **Butter the Bread:**
    - Spread a thin layer of softened butter on one side of each heart-shaped bread piece. If using mayonnaise, you can spread it on the other side for extra creaminess.
3. **Assemble the Sandwiches:**
    - Place half of the heart-shaped bread slices butter-side down on a clean surface.
    - Sprinkle a generous amount of shredded cheese on each of these bread slices. Add any additional fillings if desired.
    - Top with the remaining bread slices, butter-side up, to create the sandwiches.
4. **Cook the Sandwiches:**
    - Heat a non-stick skillet or griddle over medium heat.
    - Place the sandwiches in the skillet and cook for 2-3 minutes on each side, or until the bread is golden brown and the cheese is melted. Press down slightly with a spatula to ensure even toasting and melting.
5. **Serve:**
    - Remove the sandwiches from the skillet and let them cool for a minute before serving. Cut the sandwiches in half if desired and serve with a side of tomato soup or a simple salad.

Tips:

- **Cheese Choice:** Experiment with different cheeses or cheese blends for varied flavors and textures.
- **Additions:** For extra flavor, try adding a layer of caramelized onions, cooked bacon, or tomato slices inside the sandwich before grilling.
- **Cooking:** Make sure to cook over medium heat to allow the cheese to melt properly without burning the bread.

Heart-Shaped Grilled Cheese Sandwiches are not only cute but also a comforting and tasty lunch option. Enjoy this delightful recipe with your loved ones for a memorable and delicious meal!

Roasted Red Pepper and Tomato Soup

Ingredients:

- 4 large red bell peppers
- 6 ripe tomatoes, quartered
- 1 medium onion, chopped
- 3 cloves garlic, minced
- 2 tablespoons olive oil
- 4 cups vegetable or chicken broth
- 1 teaspoon dried basil
- 1/2 teaspoon dried thyme
- 1/2 teaspoon smoked paprika
- Salt and pepper to taste
- 1/4 cup heavy cream (optional for creaminess)
- Fresh basil leaves or parsley for garnish

Instructions:

1. **Roast the Peppers and Tomatoes:**
   - Preheat your oven to 400°F (200°C).
   - Place the red bell peppers and quartered tomatoes on a baking sheet. Drizzle with 1 tablespoon of olive oil and toss to coat.
   - Roast in the preheated oven for 30-35 minutes, or until the peppers are charred and the tomatoes are soft and caramelized. Remove from the oven and let cool slightly.
2. **Peel and Prep the Peppers:**
   - Once the peppers are cool enough to handle, peel off the charred skin, remove the seeds, and cut them into strips. Set aside.
   - If desired, peel the tomatoes, but this is optional as the skin can be blended into the soup.
3. **Sauté the Aromatics:**
   - In a large pot, heat the remaining 1 tablespoon of olive oil over medium heat.
   - Add the chopped onion and sauté for 5-7 minutes, or until translucent and softened.
   - Add the minced garlic and cook for another 1-2 minutes, until fragrant.
4. **Blend the Soup:**
   - Add the roasted peppers and tomatoes to the pot with the onions and garlic.
   - Pour in the vegetable or chicken broth.
   - Stir in the dried basil, thyme, smoked paprika, salt, and pepper.
   - Bring the mixture to a simmer and cook for 10-15 minutes to allow the flavors to meld.
   - Use an immersion blender to puree the soup until smooth. Alternatively, you can carefully transfer the soup in batches to a blender.
5. **Finish the Soup:**

- If you prefer a creamier soup, stir in the heavy cream and heat through.
- Adjust the seasoning with more salt and pepper, if needed.
6. **Serve:**
    - Ladle the soup into bowls and garnish with fresh basil leaves or parsley.
    - Serve hot with a side of crusty bread or grilled cheese sandwiches.

Tips:

- **Roasting:** Ensure the peppers and tomatoes are well-roasted to enhance their natural sweetness and depth of flavor.
- **Creaminess:** For a vegan option, you can omit the heavy cream or substitute with coconut milk or a splash of almond milk.
- **Spice Level:** Adjust the seasoning to your taste, adding a pinch of red pepper flakes for extra heat if desired.

This Roasted Red Pepper and Tomato Soup is a delightful, hearty meal that pairs wonderfully with a variety of side dishes and makes for a comforting lunch or dinner option. Enjoy the rich, roasted flavors and the warmth it brings to your table!

Strawberry Spinach Salad with Poppy Seed Dressing

Ingredients:

For the Salad:

- 6 cups fresh baby spinach leaves
- 1 cup fresh strawberries, hulled and sliced
- 1/4 cup red onion, thinly sliced
- 1/4 cup crumbled feta cheese or goat cheese
- 1/4 cup sliced almonds or pecans (toasted, if desired)
- 1/4 cup thinly sliced cucumber (optional)
- 1/4 cup cooked chicken breast, sliced (optional, for added protein)

For the Poppy Seed Dressing:

- 1/4 cup mayonnaise
- 1/4 cup plain Greek yogurt (or more mayonnaise, if preferred)
- 2 tablespoons honey
- 2 tablespoons apple cider vinegar
- 1 tablespoon poppy seeds
- 1 tablespoon Dijon mustard
- Salt and pepper to taste

Instructions:

1. **Prepare the Salad Ingredients:**
   - In a large salad bowl, combine the fresh baby spinach leaves, sliced strawberries, red onion, and optional cucumber and chicken.
   - Sprinkle the crumbled feta or goat cheese and sliced almonds or pecans over the top.
2. **Make the Poppy Seed Dressing:**
   - In a small bowl, whisk together the mayonnaise, Greek yogurt, honey, apple cider vinegar, poppy seeds, and Dijon mustard until smooth and well combined.
   - Season with salt and pepper to taste. Adjust the sweetness or acidity as needed by adding more honey or vinegar.
3. **Toss the Salad:**
   - Just before serving, drizzle the poppy seed dressing over the salad.
   - Gently toss to coat the ingredients evenly with the dressing.
4. **Serve:**
   - Serve the salad immediately for the freshest taste, or keep the dressing on the side if preparing in advance.

Tips:

- **Cheese Choices:** You can substitute feta with goat cheese, blue cheese, or even shredded Parmesan based on your preference.
- **Nuts:** Toasting the nuts can enhance their flavor and crunchiness.
- **Chicken:** Adding grilled chicken breast makes this salad a complete meal and adds protein.
- **Dressing Storage:** Store any leftover dressing in an airtight container in the refrigerator for up to a week. Shake well before using.

This **Strawberry Spinach Salad with Poppy Seed Dressing** is a delightful combination of sweet, savory, and tangy flavors, making it a perfect choice for a refreshing and satisfying meal. Enjoy the fresh and vibrant taste of this salad any time of the year!

Love-Infused Chicken Caesar Wraps

Ingredients:

For the Chicken:

- 2 boneless, skinless chicken breasts
- 2 tablespoons olive oil
- 1 teaspoon garlic powder
- 1 teaspoon onion powder
- 1/2 teaspoon dried oregano
- Salt and pepper to taste

For the Wraps:

- 4 large flour tortillas (or whole wheat tortillas, if preferred)
- 2 cups chopped romaine lettuce
- 1/2 cup grated Parmesan cheese
- 1/4 cup Caesar dressing (store-bought or homemade)
- Optional: Croutons for extra crunch

For the Homemade Caesar Dressing (optional):

- 1/2 cup mayonnaise
- 1/4 cup grated Parmesan cheese
- 1 tablespoon lemon juice
- 1 tablespoon Dijon mustard
- 1 clove garlic, minced
- 1 teaspoon anchovy paste (optional)
- Salt and pepper to taste

Instructions:

1. **Prepare the Chicken:**
   - Preheat your grill or a skillet over medium-high heat.
   - Brush the chicken breasts with olive oil and season with garlic powder, onion powder, dried oregano, salt, and pepper.
   - Grill or cook the chicken for 6-8 minutes per side, or until the internal temperature reaches 165°F (74°C) and the chicken is cooked through.
   - Remove the chicken from the heat and let it rest for a few minutes before slicing into thin strips.
2. **Prepare the Caesar Dressing (if making homemade):**
   - In a small bowl, whisk together the mayonnaise, grated Parmesan cheese, lemon juice, Dijon mustard, minced garlic, and anchovy paste (if using).
   - Season with salt and pepper to taste.
3. **Assemble the Wraps:**

- Lay out the tortillas on a flat surface.
- Spread a spoonful of Caesar dressing in the center of each tortilla.
- Layer on the chopped romaine lettuce, sliced chicken, and grated Parmesan cheese.
- Add croutons if desired for extra crunch.

4. **Wrap and Serve:**
   - Fold in the sides of the tortilla and roll it up from the bottom to enclose the filling.
   - Slice the wraps in half diagonally if desired, and serve immediately.

Tips:

- **Chicken Variations:** For extra flavor, marinate the chicken in Caesar dressing for a few hours before grilling.
- **Tortilla Choices:** You can use whole wheat or spinach tortillas for added nutrition and color.
- **Crunch Factor:** Adding croutons to the wrap provides a nice crunch but is optional if you prefer a softer texture.

Love-Infused Chicken Caesar Wraps are a tasty and practical way to enjoy the classic flavors of a Caesar salad, with the added convenience of a handheld meal. Enjoy these wraps as a satisfying lunch, a quick dinner, or a flavorful picnic option!

Creamy Avocado and Tuna Salad

Ingredients:

- 1 can (5 oz) tuna, drained (use white albacore or chunk light)
- 1 ripe avocado, peeled, pitted, and diced
- 1/4 cup red onion, finely chopped
- 1/4 cup celery, finely chopped
- 2 tablespoons fresh parsley, chopped
- 2 tablespoons Greek yogurt or mayonnaise
- 1 tablespoon lemon juice
- 1 teaspoon Dijon mustard
- Salt and pepper to taste
- Optional: 1 tablespoon capers, chopped

Instructions:

1. **Prepare the Ingredients:**
   - In a medium bowl, combine the drained tuna, diced avocado, chopped red onion, chopped celery, and parsley.
2. **Make the Dressing:**
   - In a small bowl, mix together the Greek yogurt or mayonnaise, lemon juice, Dijon mustard, salt, and pepper.
3. **Combine and Mix:**
   - Gently fold the dressing into the tuna and avocado mixture until well combined. Be careful not to mash the avocado too much; it should remain chunky for texture.
4. **Add Optional Ingredients:**
   - If using, fold in the chopped capers for an extra burst of flavor.
5. **Serve:**
   - Serve the creamy avocado and tuna salad on a bed of greens, in a sandwich, or in a wrap. It also pairs well with whole-grain crackers or as a topping for toast.

Tips:

- **Avocado:** Choose a ripe avocado that is soft but not mushy for the best texture and flavor.
- **Tuna:** For a healthier option, use tuna packed in water rather than oil. If you prefer, you can use fresh tuna steak, cooked and flaked.
- **Make Ahead:** This salad can be made ahead of time and stored in an airtight container in the refrigerator for up to 1-2 days. However, it's best enjoyed fresh to prevent the avocado from browning.

Creamy Avocado and Tuna Salad is a delicious and wholesome meal that combines creamy avocado with flavorful tuna and fresh vegetables. It's a perfect choice for a quick and nutritious lunch or light dinner!

Sweetheart Caprese Salad

Ingredients:

- 2 cups cherry or grape tomatoes, halved
- 8 ounces fresh mozzarella balls (bocconcini or ciliegine), drained
- 1/4 cup fresh basil leaves
- 2 tablespoons extra-virgin olive oil
- 1 tablespoon balsamic glaze or reduction
- Salt and freshly ground black pepper to taste
- Optional: 1 teaspoon dried oregano or Italian seasoning for extra flavor

Instructions:

1. **Prepare the Ingredients:**
   - **Tomatoes:** Slice the cherry or grape tomatoes in half. If using larger tomatoes, cut them into bite-sized pieces.
   - **Mozzarella:** Drain the mozzarella balls and pat them dry with a paper towel.
   - **Basil:** Gently tear the fresh basil leaves into smaller pieces or leave them whole for a rustic look.
2. **Form Heart Shapes (Optional):**
   - To create heart shapes, use a small heart-shaped cookie cutter to cut out slices of mozzarella. If you don't have a cookie cutter, you can slice the mozzarella into small rounds and arrange them in a heart shape on the plate.
3. **Assemble the Salad:**
   - Arrange the tomato halves and mozzarella balls on a serving platter or individual plates.
   - Tuck basil leaves in between the tomatoes and mozzarella.
4. **Season and Dress:**
   - Drizzle the extra-virgin olive oil and balsamic glaze over the salad.
   - Sprinkle with salt, freshly ground black pepper, and optional dried oregano or Italian seasoning.
5. **Serve:**
   - Serve immediately as a fresh and vibrant starter or side dish.

Tips:

- **Balsamic Glaze:** You can make a balsamic glaze by reducing balsamic vinegar in a saucepan over medium heat until it thickens. Let it cool before drizzling.
- **Cheese Variations:** If you prefer, you can use a large ball of fresh mozzarella and slice it into rounds.
- **Tomato Choices:** Mix different types of tomatoes for added color and flavor.

Sweetheart Caprese Salad is not only a feast for the eyes but also for the taste buds. The combination of sweet tomatoes, creamy mozzarella, and aromatic basil, paired with a drizzle of olive oil and balsamic glaze, makes this salad a perfect choice for a romantic meal or any special occasion. Enjoy this charming and delicious salad as part of your celebration!

Spicy Shrimp Tacos with Cilantro Lime Slaw

Ingredients:

For the Spicy Shrimp:

- 1 pound large shrimp, peeled and deveined
- 2 tablespoons olive oil
- 1 tablespoon smoked paprika
- 1 teaspoon ground cumin
- 1 teaspoon garlic powder
- 1/2 teaspoon cayenne pepper (adjust to taste)
- 1/2 teaspoon chili powder
- Salt and freshly ground black pepper to taste
- Juice of 1 lime

For the Cilantro Lime Slaw:

- 4 cups shredded cabbage (mix of green and red cabbage)
- 1 cup shredded carrots
- 1/4 cup fresh cilantro, chopped
- 1/4 cup mayonnaise
- 2 tablespoons lime juice
- 1 tablespoon honey or agave syrup
- 1/2 teaspoon ground cumin
- Salt and freshly ground black pepper to taste

For the Tacos:

- 8 small corn or flour tortillas
- 1 avocado, sliced
- Lime wedges for serving
- Fresh cilantro leaves for garnish

Instructions:

1. **Prepare the Shrimp:**
   - In a large bowl, toss the shrimp with olive oil, smoked paprika, ground cumin, garlic powder, cayenne pepper, chili powder, salt, and pepper until evenly coated.
   - Heat a large skillet over medium-high heat. Cook the shrimp for 2-3 minutes per side, or until they are pink and opaque. Remove from heat and squeeze lime juice over the cooked shrimp.
2. **Make the Cilantro Lime Slaw:**
   - In a large bowl, combine the shredded cabbage, shredded carrots, and chopped cilantro.

- In a separate small bowl, whisk together the mayonnaise, lime juice, honey or agave syrup, ground cumin, salt, and pepper.
- Pour the dressing over the cabbage mixture and toss until well coated. Adjust seasoning to taste.

3. **Warm the Tortillas:**
    - Heat the tortillas in a dry skillet over medium heat for about 30 seconds per side, or until they are warm and pliable. Alternatively, you can wrap them in foil and heat them in the oven.
4. **Assemble the Tacos:**
    - Spread a spoonful of cilantro lime slaw on each tortilla.
    - Top with the spicy shrimp.
    - Add a few slices of avocado.
    - Garnish with extra cilantro leaves and serve with lime wedges on the side.
5. **Serve:**
    - Serve the tacos immediately while the tortillas are warm and the shrimp are fresh.

Tips:

- **Spicy Level:** Adjust the amount of cayenne pepper based on your spice tolerance.
- **Slaw Variations:** Add sliced jalapeños or radishes to the slaw for extra crunch and heat.
- **Tortilla Choices:** Use corn tortillas for a more traditional flavor or flour tortillas for a softer texture.

Spicy Shrimp Tacos with Cilantro Lime Slaw offer a delicious blend of spicy, tangy, and creamy flavors that make for an irresistible meal. These tacos are perfect for a casual dinner or a festive gathering, bringing a burst of flavor and color to your table. Enjoy!

Heart-Shaped Pizza Pockets

Ingredients:

For the Dough:

- 1 package (14 ounces) refrigerated pizza dough (store-bought) or homemade pizza dough
- Flour, for dusting

For the Filling:

- 1 cup pizza sauce or marinara sauce
- 1 1/2 cups shredded mozzarella cheese
- 1/2 cup sliced pepperoni, cooked sausage, or your choice of pizza toppings (such as mushrooms, bell peppers, olives, etc.)
- 1/4 cup grated Parmesan cheese (optional)
- 1 teaspoon dried oregano
- 1/2 teaspoon garlic powder

For the Egg Wash:

- 1 egg, beaten with 1 tablespoon water

For Garnish:

- Fresh basil or parsley, chopped (optional)

Instructions:

1. **Prepare the Dough:**
   - Preheat your oven to 400°F (200°C).
   - Lightly flour a clean surface and roll out the pizza dough into a thin rectangle.
2. **Cut the Dough:**
   - Use a heart-shaped cookie cutter to cut out heart shapes from the dough. If you don't have a cookie cutter, you can use a knife to cut out heart shapes freehand.
   - You should have an even number of heart shapes to make the pockets.
3. **Assemble the Pizza Pockets:**
   - Place half of the heart-shaped dough pieces on a baking sheet lined with parchment paper.
   - Spread a spoonful of pizza sauce on each piece, leaving a small border around the edges.
   - Sprinkle with shredded mozzarella cheese, and add your choice of toppings. If using, sprinkle a bit of grated Parmesan cheese over the top.
   - Sprinkle the filling with dried oregano and garlic powder for added flavor.
4. **Seal the Pockets:**

- Place the remaining heart-shaped dough pieces on top of the filled ones to create pockets. Press the edges together to seal, using a fork to crimp the edges if desired.
5. **Brush and Bake:**
    - Brush the tops of the pizza pockets with the beaten egg wash to give them a golden, glossy finish.
    - Bake in the preheated oven for 12-15 minutes, or until the dough is golden brown and the cheese is melted and bubbly.
6. **Serve:**
    - Allow the pizza pockets to cool slightly before serving. Garnish with fresh basil or parsley if desired.

Tips:

- **Dough:** If using homemade dough, roll it out thinly for a crispier pocket.
- **Filling:** Be creative with your fillings—try different cheeses, meats, and vegetables to suit your taste.
- **Sealing:** Make sure the edges are well sealed to prevent any filling from leaking out during baking.

Heart-Shaped Pizza Pockets are a delightful and customizable treat that adds a touch of romance and fun to your pizza night. Enjoy these delicious pockets with a side of marinara sauce for dipping or as part of a festive meal!

Mediterranean Quinoa Salad

Ingredients:

For the Salad:

- 1 cup quinoa (uncooked)
- 2 cups water or vegetable broth
- 1 cup cherry or grape tomatoes, halved
- 1 cup cucumber, diced
- 1/2 cup red onion, finely chopped
- 1/2 cup Kalamata olives or black olives, pitted and sliced
- 1/2 cup crumbled feta cheese
- 1/4 cup fresh parsley, chopped
- 1/4 cup fresh mint leaves, chopped (optional)
- 1 avocado, diced (optional)

For the Lemon Vinaigrette:

- 1/4 cup extra-virgin olive oil
- 2 tablespoons lemon juice (freshly squeezed)
- 1 teaspoon Dijon mustard
- 1 clove garlic, minced
- 1/2 teaspoon dried oregano
- Salt and freshly ground black pepper to taste

Instructions:

1. **Cook the Quinoa:**
   - Rinse the quinoa under cold water to remove any bitterness.
   - In a medium saucepan, bring 2 cups of water or vegetable broth to a boil.
   - Add the quinoa, reduce heat to low, cover, and simmer for about 15 minutes, or until the quinoa is cooked and the liquid is absorbed.
   - Remove from heat and let it sit covered for 5 minutes. Fluff with a fork and let it cool to room temperature.
2. **Prepare the Vegetables:**
   - While the quinoa is cooling, prepare the tomatoes, cucumber, red onion, olives, and any optional ingredients like avocado and fresh herbs.
3. **Make the Lemon Vinaigrette:**
   - In a small bowl, whisk together the olive oil, lemon juice, Dijon mustard, minced garlic, dried oregano, salt, and pepper until well combined.
4. **Assemble the Salad:**
   - In a large bowl, combine the cooled quinoa, tomatoes, cucumber, red onion, olives, feta cheese, parsley, and mint.
   - Pour the lemon vinaigrette over the salad and toss gently to combine.

5. **Serve:**
   - Serve the salad immediately, or refrigerate it for about 30 minutes to let the flavors meld together. If adding avocado, toss it in just before serving to prevent browning.

Tips:

- **Quinoa Variations:** You can use different types of quinoa, such as red or black quinoa, for added texture and color.
- **Protein Addition:** Add grilled chicken, chickpeas, or other protein sources if you want to make this salad a more substantial meal.
- **Storage:** Store any leftover salad in an airtight container in the refrigerator for up to 3-4 days.

Mediterranean Quinoa Salad is a versatile and flavorful dish that's both healthy and satisfying. Enjoy this refreshing salad as a side dish or a main course, and savor the vibrant Mediterranean flavors in every bite!

Roasted Beet and Goat Cheese Salad

Ingredients:

For the Salad:

- 4 medium beets, scrubbed and trimmed
- 2 tablespoons olive oil
- Salt and freshly ground black pepper to taste
- 4 cups mixed salad greens (such as arugula, spinach, and baby greens)
- 1/4 cup crumbled goat cheese
- 1/4 cup walnuts or pecans, toasted (optional)
- 1/4 cup thinly sliced red onion (optional)
- 1 apple or pear, thinly sliced (optional, for added sweetness)
- Fresh herbs for garnish (optional, such as parsley or chives)

For the Balsamic Vinaigrette:

- 1/4 cup balsamic vinegar
- 2 tablespoons extra-virgin olive oil
- 1 tablespoon honey or maple syrup
- 1 teaspoon Dijon mustard
- 1 clove garlic, minced
- Salt and freshly ground black pepper to taste

Instructions:

1. **Roast the Beets:**
    - Preheat your oven to 400°F (200°C).
    - Wrap each beet individually in aluminum foil and place them on a baking sheet.
    - Roast the beets for 45-60 minutes, or until they are tender when pierced with a fork.
    - Remove from the oven and let cool slightly. Once cool enough to handle, peel the beets (the skin should come off easily) and cut them into wedges or bite-sized pieces.
2. **Make the Balsamic Vinaigrette:**
    - In a small bowl, whisk together the balsamic vinegar, olive oil, honey or maple syrup, Dijon mustard, minced garlic, salt, and pepper until well combined. Adjust the seasoning to taste.
3. **Assemble the Salad:**
    - In a large bowl, toss the mixed salad greens with a small amount of the balsamic vinaigrette.
    - Arrange the roasted beet pieces on top of the greens.
    - Sprinkle with crumbled goat cheese, toasted walnuts or pecans (if using), and thinly sliced red onion (if using).

- Add apple or pear slices for a touch of sweetness, if desired.
4. **Serve:**
    - Drizzle with additional balsamic vinaigrette if needed and toss gently to combine.
    - Garnish with fresh herbs, if desired.

Tips:

- **Beet Preparation:** You can also use pre-cooked beets from the store to save time, just make sure to adjust the cooking time accordingly.
- **Nut Options:** For added texture and flavor, try different nuts or seeds, such as pumpkin seeds or almonds.
- **Vinaigrette Variations:** Experiment with different types of vinegar (e.g., red wine vinegar) or add a touch of mustard for a different twist on the vinaigrette.

Roasted Beet and Goat Cheese Salad combines rich, roasted beets with creamy goat cheese and crunchy nuts, all balanced by a tangy balsamic vinaigrette. This salad is not only visually appealing but also packed with flavor, making it a perfect choice for a special meal or a sophisticated side dish. Enjoy!

Heart-Shaped Beet and Hummus Sandwiches

Ingredients:

For the Sandwiches:

- 4 slices of bread (whole grain, sourdough, or your choice)
- 1 cup roasted beets, sliced (recipe below)
- 1/2 cup hummus (store-bought or homemade)
- 1/4 cup fresh arugula or spinach
- 1/4 cup crumbled feta cheese (optional)
- 1 tablespoon olive oil
- Salt and freshly ground black pepper to taste

For the Roasted Beets:

- 2 medium beets, scrubbed and trimmed
- 1 tablespoon olive oil
- Salt and freshly ground black pepper to taste

Instructions:

1. **Prepare the Roasted Beets:**
    - Preheat your oven to 400°F (200°C).
    - Wrap each beet individually in aluminum foil and place them on a baking sheet.
    - Roast the beets for 45-60 minutes, or until they are tender when pierced with a fork.
    - Remove from the oven and let cool slightly. Once cool enough to handle, peel the beets (the skin should come off easily) and slice them into thin rounds or half-moons.
2. **Prepare the Bread:**
    - Using a heart-shaped cookie cutter, cut out heart shapes from each slice of bread. You should get two hearts per slice of bread if using a small cutter.
3. **Assemble the Sandwiches:**
    - Spread a generous layer of hummus on one side of each heart-shaped bread piece.
    - Layer roasted beet slices on top of the hummus. Drizzle lightly with olive oil and season with salt and pepper.
    - Add a handful of fresh arugula or spinach on top of the beets.
    - If using, sprinkle crumbled feta cheese over the arugula.
    - Top with another heart-shaped bread slice, hummus side down, to complete the sandwich.
4. **Serve:**
    - Arrange the sandwiches on a serving platter. For a touch of elegance, you can cut the sandwiches into smaller halves or quarters.

- Serve immediately or wrap them in parchment paper for a packed lunch.

Tips:

- **Hummus Varieties:** Feel free to use different flavors of hummus, such as roasted red pepper or spicy harissa, for added flavor.
- **Beet Slicing:** Slice the beets thinly to make them easier to layer in the sandwiches.
- **Bread Options:** Use your favorite type of bread, and consider toasting it lightly for extra crunch.

Heart-Shaped Beet and Hummus Sandwiches are a whimsical and healthy option that adds a touch of romance to any meal. Enjoy these sandwiches for a delightful lunch or snack, and savor the combination of roasted beets, creamy hummus, and fresh greens all wrapped in a fun, heart-shaped package!

Chicken and Strawberry Salad with Balsamic Vinaigrette

Ingredients:

For the Salad:

- 2 boneless, skinless chicken breasts
- 1 tablespoon olive oil
- Salt and freshly ground black pepper to taste
- 6 cups mixed salad greens (such as spinach, arugula, and baby greens)
- 1 cup fresh strawberries, hulled and sliced
- 1/4 cup crumbled feta cheese or goat cheese
- 1/4 cup sliced almonds or walnuts, toasted (optional)
- 1/4 red onion, thinly sliced (optional)

For the Balsamic Vinaigrette:

- 1/4 cup balsamic vinegar
- 2 tablespoons extra-virgin olive oil
- 1 tablespoon honey or maple syrup
- 1 teaspoon Dijon mustard
- 1 clove garlic, minced
- Salt and freshly ground black pepper to taste

Instructions:

1. **Cook the Chicken:**
    - Preheat your grill or a skillet over medium-high heat.
    - Brush the chicken breasts with olive oil and season with salt and pepper.
    - Grill or cook the chicken for 6-7 minutes per side, or until fully cooked and the internal temperature reaches 165°F (75°C). The chicken should be golden brown and juices should run clear.
    - Remove from heat and let the chicken rest for a few minutes before slicing it into thin strips or bite-sized pieces.
2. **Prepare the Balsamic Vinaigrette:**
    - In a small bowl, whisk together the balsamic vinegar, olive oil, honey or maple syrup, Dijon mustard, minced garlic, salt, and pepper until well combined. Adjust seasoning to taste.
3. **Assemble the Salad:**
    - In a large salad bowl, combine the mixed salad greens, sliced strawberries, and red onion (if using).
    - Arrange the sliced chicken on top of the salad.
    - Sprinkle with crumbled feta cheese or goat cheese and toasted almonds or walnuts (if using).
4. **Dress the Salad:**

- Drizzle the balsamic vinaigrette over the salad just before serving. Toss gently to coat all ingredients with the dressing.
5. **Serve:**
    - Serve immediately to enjoy the freshness of the ingredients.

Tips:

- **Chicken Variations:** You can use grilled, baked, or even shredded rotisserie chicken for convenience.
- **Strawberries:** For a more festive touch, you can also use other berries like blueberries or raspberries.
- **Nuts:** Toast the nuts lightly for extra flavor and crunch.

Chicken and Strawberry Salad with Balsamic Vinaigrette combines the juicy sweetness of strawberries with savory chicken and a tangy vinaigrette, making it a perfect choice for a light yet satisfying meal. This salad is both nutritious and flavorful, ideal for enjoying during the warmer months or any time you crave a refreshing meal.

Smoked Salmon and Cream Cheese Crostini

Ingredients:

For the Crostini:

- 1 baguette, sliced into 1/2-inch thick slices
- 2 tablespoons olive oil
- 1 garlic clove, peeled (optional)

For the Topping:

- 8 ounces cream cheese, softened
- 2 tablespoons fresh dill, chopped (plus extra for garnish)
- 1 tablespoon lemon juice
- 1/2 teaspoon lemon zest (optional)
- 4 ounces smoked salmon, thinly sliced
- Capers (optional, for garnish)
- Freshly ground black pepper, to taste

Instructions:

1. **Prepare the Crostini:**
    - Preheat your oven to 400°F (200°C).
    - Arrange the baguette slices in a single layer on a baking sheet.
    - Brush each slice lightly with olive oil.
    - Toast in the preheated oven for 5-7 minutes, or until the slices are golden and crisp.
    - Optional: Rub each toasted baguette slice with the cut side of the garlic clove for a subtle garlic flavor.
2. **Prepare the Cream Cheese Spread:**
    - In a medium bowl, mix together the softened cream cheese, chopped dill, lemon juice, and lemon zest (if using) until well combined. Season with freshly ground black pepper to taste.
3. **Assemble the Crostini:**
    - Spread a generous layer of the cream cheese mixture onto each toasted baguette slice.
    - Top with a slice or piece of smoked salmon.
    - Garnish with additional fresh dill and capers (if using).
4. **Serve:**
    - Arrange the crostini on a serving platter and serve immediately.

Tips:

- **Cream Cheese Variations:** For added flavor, you can mix in some chopped chives, garlic, or horseradish into the cream cheese spread.
- **Smoked Salmon Alternatives:** If you prefer, you can use gravlax or another type of cured fish.
- **Crostini Storage:** If preparing in advance, store the toasted baguette slices and the cream cheese mixture separately to keep everything fresh and crisp. Assemble just before serving.

Smoked Salmon and Cream Cheese Crostini offer a delightful blend of creamy, smoky, and tangy flavors on a crunchy base. These crostini are perfect for entertaining, adding a touch of elegance to any occasion. Enjoy these delicious bites as a sophisticated appetizer or a delightful snack!

Spinach and Feta Stuffed Chicken Breasts

Ingredients:

For the Stuffing:

- 1 cup fresh spinach, chopped
- 1/2 cup crumbled feta cheese
- 1/4 cup grated Parmesan cheese
- 2 tablespoons sun-dried tomatoes, chopped (optional)
- 1 clove garlic, minced
- 1 tablespoon olive oil
- Salt and freshly ground black pepper to taste

For the Chicken:

- 4 boneless, skinless chicken breasts
- 2 tablespoons olive oil
- 1 teaspoon dried oregano
- 1 teaspoon dried thyme
- 1/2 teaspoon paprika
- Salt and freshly ground black pepper to taste
- Toothpicks or kitchen twine for securing (optional)

Instructions:

1. **Prepare the Stuffing:**
   - In a medium skillet, heat 1 tablespoon of olive oil over medium heat.
   - Add the minced garlic and cook for about 1 minute until fragrant.
   - Add the chopped spinach and cook until wilted, about 2-3 minutes.
   - Remove from heat and let cool slightly.
   - In a bowl, combine the cooked spinach, crumbled feta cheese, grated Parmesan cheese, sun-dried tomatoes (if using), salt, and pepper. Mix well.
2. **Prepare the Chicken:**
   - Preheat your oven to 375°F (190°C).
   - Place the chicken breasts on a cutting board and use a sharp knife to create a pocket in each chicken breast by slicing horizontally, but not all the way through.
   - Season the chicken breasts on both sides with salt, pepper, dried oregano, dried thyme, and paprika.
   - Stuff each chicken breast with the spinach and feta mixture, using toothpicks or kitchen twine to secure the openings if necessary.
3. **Cook the Chicken:**
   - Heat 2 tablespoons of olive oil in a large oven-proof skillet over medium-high heat.

- Add the stuffed chicken breasts and sear for about 3-4 minutes on each side, until golden brown.
- Transfer the skillet to the preheated oven and bake for 20-25 minutes, or until the chicken reaches an internal temperature of 165°F (74°C) and is cooked through.

4. **Serve:**
    - Remove the chicken from the oven and let it rest for a few minutes before removing the toothpicks or twine.
    - Slice the chicken breasts and serve with your choice of side dishes, such as roasted vegetables, quinoa, or a simple salad.

Tips:

- **Spinach Preparation:** Ensure the spinach is well-drained after cooking to avoid excess moisture in the stuffing.
- **Cheese Variations:** You can substitute the feta cheese with goat cheese or ricotta if you prefer.
- **Chicken Tenderness:** If the chicken breasts are very thick, you can pound them slightly to ensure even cooking.

Spinach and Feta Stuffed Chicken Breasts are a delicious and impressive dish that combines tender chicken with a flavorful spinach and feta filling. This recipe is perfect for a special occasion or a comforting weeknight dinner, offering a great balance of taste and nutrition. Enjoy this dish with your favorite sides for a complete and satisfying meal!

Mini Heart-Shaped Quiches

Ingredients:

For the Crust:

- 1 package (14 ounces) refrigerated pie crusts (or homemade pie crust)
- Flour, for dusting

For the Filling:

- 4 large eggs
- 1/2 cup milk or cream
- 1/2 cup shredded cheese (cheddar, Swiss, or your choice)
- 1/2 cup cooked and crumbled bacon, sausage, or diced ham (optional)
- 1/2 cup fresh spinach, chopped (or other vegetables like bell peppers, mushrooms, or onions)
- Salt and freshly ground black pepper to taste
- 1/4 teaspoon dried thyme or oregano (optional)
- Fresh herbs for garnish (optional, such as chives or parsley)

Instructions:

1. **Prepare the Crust:**
    - Preheat your oven to 375°F (190°C).
    - Roll out the pie crusts on a lightly floured surface.
    - Using a heart-shaped cookie cutter, cut out heart shapes from the pie crusts.
    - Gently press the heart-shaped crusts into the wells of a mini muffin tin or tartlet pan, pressing down lightly to fit.
2. **Prepare the Filling:**
    - In a medium bowl, whisk together the eggs and milk or cream until well combined.
    - Stir in the shredded cheese, cooked bacon or sausage (if using), chopped spinach, salt, pepper, and dried thyme or oregano.
    - Mix well to ensure all ingredients are evenly distributed.
3. **Assemble the Quiches:**
    - Spoon the egg mixture into each heart-shaped crust, filling each about 2/3 full.
    - If desired, top with additional cheese or herbs for extra flavor.
4. **Bake the Quiches:**
    - Place the muffin tin or tartlet pan in the preheated oven.
    - Bake for 15-20 minutes, or until the quiches are set in the center and the crust is golden brown.
    - Remove from the oven and let the quiches cool slightly before removing from the pan.
5. **Serve:**

- Garnish with fresh herbs if desired.
- Serve warm or at room temperature.

Tips:

- **Crust Alternatives:** You can use store-bought phyllo dough or puff pastry for a different texture, or make a gluten-free crust if needed.
- **Filling Variations:** Customize the quiches with your favorite vegetables, cheeses, or meats. You can also make a vegetarian version by omitting meat and adding extra vegetables.
- **Make-Ahead:** Mini quiches can be made ahead and stored in the refrigerator for up to 3 days, or frozen for up to 1 month. Reheat in a 350°F (175°C) oven until warmed through.

Mini Heart-Shaped Quiches are a charming and versatile option for any meal or event. With their cute heart shape and savory filling, these quiches are sure to be a hit with everyone. Enjoy them fresh from the oven or as a make-ahead treat!

Lobster and Avocado Toast

Ingredients:

For the Toast:

- 4 slices of crusty bread (such as sourdough, ciabatta, or baguette)
- 2 tablespoons olive oil
- 1 garlic clove, peeled (optional)

For the Lobster:

- 1 lobster tail (about 6-8 ounces), cooked and shelled
- 1 tablespoon butter
- 1 teaspoon lemon juice
- 1/4 teaspoon smoked paprika or Old Bay seasoning
- Salt and freshly ground black pepper to taste

For the Avocado Spread:

- 2 ripe avocados
- 1 tablespoon lemon juice
- Salt and freshly ground black pepper to taste
- 1/4 teaspoon red pepper flakes or hot sauce (optional)

For Garnish:

- Fresh herbs, such as parsley or chives, chopped
- Lemon wedges
- Microgreens or arugula (optional)

Instructions:

1. **Prepare the Toast:**
    - Preheat your oven to 375°F (190°C).
    - Brush each slice of bread with olive oil on both sides.
    - Place the bread slices on a baking sheet and toast in the preheated oven for 8-10 minutes, or until golden and crispy.
    - Optional: Rub each toasted slice with the cut side of the garlic clove for a subtle garlic flavor.
2. **Prepare the Lobster:**
    - If using a pre-cooked lobster tail, ensure it's thawed and shelled. Cut the lobster meat into bite-sized pieces.
    - In a small skillet, melt the butter over medium heat.
    - Add the lobster meat and cook for 1-2 minutes, just until heated through.

- Stir in the lemon juice, smoked paprika or Old Bay seasoning, salt, and pepper. Remove from heat.
3. **Prepare the Avocado Spread:**
    - In a medium bowl, mash the avocados with a fork until smooth but still slightly chunky.
    - Stir in the lemon juice, salt, and pepper. Add red pepper flakes or hot sauce if desired for a bit of heat.
4. **Assemble the Toast:**
    - Spread a generous layer of the avocado mixture onto each slice of toasted bread.
    - Top with the warmed lobster meat.
    - Garnish with fresh herbs and lemon wedges. Add microgreens or arugula if desired for extra freshness and color.
5. **Serve:**
    - Serve immediately while the toast is still crispy and the toppings are fresh.

Tips:

- **Lobster Preparation:** If you need to cook the lobster, boil it in salted water for about 8-10 minutes, then cool and shell it. You can also use pre-cooked lobster meat from a seafood market.
- **Avocado Ripeness:** Make sure the avocados are ripe for a creamy texture. If you're preparing the avocado spread in advance, add a little extra lemon juice to help prevent browning.
- **Bread Choices:** For added flavor, consider using a flavored or artisanal bread.

Lobster and Avocado Toast offers a decadent combination of flavors with its creamy avocado and succulent lobster, all served on crispy toast. This dish is perfect for impressing guests or enjoying a special treat.

Pesto and Sun-Dried Tomato Panini

Ingredients:

For the Panini:

- 4 ciabatta rolls or slices of rustic Italian bread
- 1/4 cup pesto (store-bought or homemade)
- 1/2 cup sun-dried tomatoes, chopped (oil-packed or dry, rehydrated)
- 1 cup shredded mozzarella cheese or provolone cheese
- 1/4 cup grated Parmesan cheese
- 1 cup baby spinach or arugula
- 2 tablespoons olive oil (for brushing)

Optional Additions:

- 1/2 cup cooked chicken breast, sliced or shredded
- 1/4 cup sliced black olives
- 1/4 cup thinly sliced red onion

Instructions:

1. **Prepare the Ingredients:**
   - If using dry sun-dried tomatoes, rehydrate them by soaking in hot water for 20 minutes, then drain and chop.
   - If adding cooked chicken, slice or shred it into thin pieces.
2. **Assemble the Panini:**
   - Cut the ciabatta rolls in half lengthwise, or use slices of Italian bread.
   - Spread a layer of pesto on the cut side of each bread slice.
   - Evenly distribute the chopped sun-dried tomatoes over the pesto.
   - Sprinkle with shredded mozzarella or provolone cheese and grated Parmesan cheese.
   - Add a layer of baby spinach or arugula.
   - If using, layer on the cooked chicken, black olives, and red onion.
3. **Grill the Panini:**
   - Preheat a panini press or a grill pan over medium heat.
   - Brush the outside of each sandwich with olive oil to ensure a golden, crispy crust.
   - Place the sandwiches on the press or grill pan.
   - If using a panini press, close the lid and grill for about 3-5 minutes, or until the bread is crispy and the cheese is melted.
   - If using a grill pan, press down with a heavy object (like a cast-iron skillet) and grill for about 3-4 minutes per side, or until the bread is golden brown and the cheese is melted.
4. **Serve:**

- Remove the panini from the press or pan and let them cool for a minute before cutting in half.
- Serve warm.

Tips:

- **Pesto Variations:** You can use different types of pesto, such as sun-dried tomato pesto or basil pesto, depending on your preference.
- **Cheese Options:** Feel free to use other cheeses like fontina, cheddar, or gouda for a different flavor profile.
- **Bread Choice:** Ensure the bread is sturdy enough to hold the fillings and toast well without becoming soggy.

Pesto and Sun-Dried Tomato Panini offers a perfect combination of rich flavors with a crispy, grilled exterior. This sandwich is versatile and can be enjoyed on its own or with a side salad or soup for a complete meal. Enjoy the delicious blend of pesto, sun-dried tomatoes, and melted cheese in every bite!

Creamy Tomato Basil Pasta

Ingredients:

For the Pasta:

- 12 ounces pasta (penne, fettuccine, or your choice)
- Salt, for pasta water

For the Sauce:

- 2 tablespoons olive oil
- 1 small onion, finely chopped
- 3 cloves garlic, minced
- 1 can (14.5 ounces) crushed tomatoes
- 1/2 cup heavy cream or half-and-half
- 1/4 cup grated Parmesan cheese
- 1 teaspoon dried basil
- 1/2 teaspoon dried oregano
- 1/4 teaspoon red pepper flakes (optional, for a touch of heat)
- Salt and freshly ground black pepper, to taste
- 1/4 cup fresh basil leaves, chopped (plus extra for garnish)

Instructions:

1. **Cook the Pasta:**
    - Bring a large pot of salted water to a boil.
    - Add the pasta and cook according to the package instructions until al dente.
    - Drain the pasta and set aside.
2. **Prepare the Sauce:**
    - In a large skillet or saucepan, heat the olive oil over medium heat.
    - Add the chopped onion and cook for about 3-4 minutes, until softened and translucent.
    - Add the minced garlic and cook for an additional 1 minute, until fragrant.
    - Pour in the crushed tomatoes and stir to combine with the onion and garlic.
    - Stir in the dried basil, dried oregano, and red pepper flakes (if using).
    - Let the tomato mixture simmer for about 5-7 minutes, allowing the flavors to meld together.
    - Reduce the heat to low and stir in the heavy cream or half-and-half. Cook for an additional 2-3 minutes until the sauce is heated through and creamy.
    - Add the grated Parmesan cheese and stir until melted and combined.
    - Season the sauce with salt and freshly ground black pepper to taste.
3. **Combine Pasta and Sauce:**
    - Add the cooked pasta to the skillet with the sauce. Toss to coat the pasta evenly with the creamy tomato sauce.

        - Stir in the chopped fresh basil.
    4. **Serve:**
        - Serve the pasta hot, garnished with additional fresh basil and extra Parmesan cheese if desired.

Tips:

- **Pasta Choice:** You can use any type of pasta you like. Penne, fettuccine, or even spaghetti work well with this creamy sauce.
- **Cream Alternatives:** For a lighter version, you can use milk instead of heavy cream or half-and-half, though the sauce may be less creamy.
- **Adding Protein:** For a heartier meal, you can add cooked chicken, shrimp, or even crispy bacon to the pasta.

Creamy Tomato Basil Pasta is a delightful and satisfying dish that blends the comforting flavors of creamy tomato sauce with the freshness of basil. It's perfect for a quick weeknight dinner or a cozy meal with loved ones. Enjoy the rich, creamy sauce with every bite of pasta!

Heart-Shaped Turkey and Swiss Sliders

Ingredients:

For the Sliders:

- 12 slider rolls or small buns
- 1 pound ground turkey
- 6 slices Swiss cheese
- 1/2 cup mayonnaise
- 1 tablespoon Dijon mustard
- 1 tablespoon fresh parsley, chopped (optional)
- Salt and freshly ground black pepper to taste

For the Topping:

- 2 tablespoons unsalted butter, melted
- 1 teaspoon garlic powder
- 1 teaspoon onion powder
- 1/2 teaspoon dried thyme
- 1 tablespoon sesame seeds (optional)

For Garnish (optional):

- Lettuce leaves
- Tomato slices
- Pickles

Instructions:

1. **Prepare the Turkey Mixture:**
   - Preheat your oven to 375°F (190°C).
   - In a large bowl, combine the ground turkey with mayonnaise, Dijon mustard, parsley (if using), salt, and pepper. Mix until well combined.
2. **Shape and Cook the Turkey Patties:**
   - Divide the turkey mixture into 12 equal portions and shape each portion into a patty slightly smaller than the slider rolls.
   - Heat a skillet or grill pan over medium heat and cook the turkey patties for about 4-5 minutes on each side, or until fully cooked and the internal temperature reaches 165°F (74°C).
3. **Prepare the Slider Rolls:**
   - Using a heart-shaped cookie cutter, cut out heart shapes from the slider rolls. If you don't have a heart-shaped cutter, you can simply cut the rolls in half.
4. **Assemble the Sliders:**
   - Place the bottom halves of the slider rolls on a baking sheet.
   - Place a slice of Swiss cheese on each roll.

- Add a cooked turkey patty on top of the cheese.
- Cover with the top halves of the slider rolls.

5. **Prepare the Topping:**
   - In a small bowl, mix the melted butter with garlic powder, onion powder, and dried thyme.
   - Brush the tops of the sliders with the seasoned butter mixture.
   - Sprinkle with sesame seeds if desired.
6. **Bake the Sliders:**
   - Bake the sliders in the preheated oven for about 10 minutes, or until the cheese is melted and the rolls are golden brown.
7. **Serve:**
   - Remove from the oven and let cool slightly.
   - Serve warm, garnished with lettuce, tomato slices, and pickles if desired.

Tips:

- **Turkey Alternatives:** You can use ground chicken or beef instead of turkey if preferred.
- **Cheese Variations:** Feel free to substitute Swiss cheese with cheddar, provolone, or your favorite cheese.
- **Adding Vegetables:** For extra flavor, you can add sautéed onions or peppers to the turkey mixture.

Heart-Shaped Turkey and Swiss Sliders are a charming and delicious way to serve mini sandwiches. Their cute shape and savory filling make them perfect for a festive occasion or a fun meal with loved ones. Enjoy these delightful sliders as a tasty and heartwarming treat!

Greek Chicken Gyros

Ingredients:

For the Chicken Marinade:

- 1 pound boneless, skinless chicken thighs or breasts
- 1/4 cup olive oil
- 3 tablespoons lemon juice (about 1 lemon)
- 3 cloves garlic, minced
- 1 tablespoon dried oregano
- 1 teaspoon ground cumin
- 1 teaspoon paprika
- 1/2 teaspoon ground coriander
- Salt and freshly ground black pepper to taste

For the Tzatziki Sauce:

- 1 cup Greek yogurt
- 1/2 cucumber, peeled, seeded, and grated
- 2 cloves garlic, minced
- 1 tablespoon lemon juice
- 1 tablespoon fresh dill, chopped (or 1 teaspoon dried dill)
- Salt and freshly ground black pepper to taste

For Serving:

- 4 pita bread or flatbreads
- 1 cup cherry tomatoes, halved
- 1/2 red onion, thinly sliced
- 1 cup shredded lettuce
- Feta cheese, crumbled (optional)
- Fresh parsley or dill for garnish (optional)

Instructions:

1. **Marinate the Chicken:**
   - In a large bowl, whisk together olive oil, lemon juice, minced garlic, oregano, cumin, paprika, coriander, salt, and pepper.
   - Add the chicken thighs or breasts to the marinade, making sure they are evenly coated.
   - Cover and refrigerate for at least 1 hour, or up to overnight for more flavor.
2. **Prepare the Tzatziki Sauce:**
   - In a medium bowl, combine Greek yogurt, grated cucumber (make sure to squeeze out excess moisture), minced garlic, lemon juice, chopped dill, salt, and pepper.

- Mix well and refrigerate until ready to use.
3. **Cook the Chicken:**
    - Preheat your grill, grill pan, or skillet over medium-high heat.
    - Remove the chicken from the marinade and cook for about 5-7 minutes per side, or until the chicken reaches an internal temperature of 165°F (74°C) and is fully cooked.
    - Let the chicken rest for a few minutes before slicing it into strips or bite-sized pieces.
4. **Prepare the Pita Bread:**
    - If desired, warm the pita bread in a dry skillet over medium heat or in the oven for a few minutes, until soft and pliable.
5. **Assemble the Gyros:**
    - Spread a generous amount of tzatziki sauce in the center of each pita bread.
    - Top with cooked chicken, cherry tomatoes, red onion, shredded lettuce, and crumbled feta cheese if using.
    - Garnish with fresh parsley or dill if desired.
6. **Serve:**
    - Fold the pita bread around the fillings to create a wrap.
    - Serve immediately while warm, or wrap in foil or parchment paper for easy eating on the go.

Tips:

- **Chicken Variations:** If you prefer, you can use chicken breasts, but thighs tend to be more tender and flavorful.
- **Vegetable Options:** Feel free to add other vegetables like cucumbers, olives, or bell peppers to your gyros.
- **Tzatziki Adjustments:** Adjust the garlic and dill in the tzatziki sauce to your taste.

Greek Chicken Gyros offer a delicious taste of Greek cuisine with tender marinated chicken, fresh veggies, and a creamy tzatziki sauce all wrapped in warm pita bread. Enjoy this flavorful dish as a hearty meal or a fun, handheld option for any occasion!

Roasted Veggie and Hummus Wraps

Ingredients:

For the Roasted Vegetables:

- 1 red bell pepper, sliced
- 1 yellow bell pepper, sliced
- 1 zucchini, sliced into rounds
- 1 red onion, sliced into wedges
- 1 cup cherry tomatoes, halved
- 2 tablespoons olive oil
- 1 teaspoon dried oregano
- 1 teaspoon dried thyme
- 1/2 teaspoon garlic powder
- Salt and freshly ground black pepper to taste

For the Hummus:

- 1 cup store-bought or homemade hummus (flavor of your choice, such as classic or roasted red pepper)
- 1 tablespoon lemon juice (optional, for extra zing)

For Assembly:

- 4 large tortillas or flatbreads (whole wheat, spinach, or your choice)
- 1 cup baby spinach or mixed greens
- 1/4 cup crumbled feta cheese (optional)
- 1/4 cup sliced black olives (optional)
- Fresh herbs for garnish (optional, such as parsley or basil)

Instructions:

1. **Roast the Vegetables:**
    - Preheat your oven to 425°F (220°C).
    - On a large baking sheet, arrange the sliced bell peppers, zucchini, red onion, and cherry tomatoes.
    - Drizzle the vegetables with olive oil and sprinkle with dried oregano, thyme, garlic powder, salt, and pepper.
    - Toss the vegetables to coat them evenly.
    - Roast in the preheated oven for 20-25 minutes, or until the vegetables are tender and slightly caramelized, stirring halfway through.
2. **Prepare the Hummus:**
    - If you'd like a tangier hummus, stir in the lemon juice to the hummus. This step is optional and can be adjusted to taste.
3. **Assemble the Wraps:**

- Lay out the tortillas or flatbreads on a clean surface.
- Spread a generous layer of hummus on each tortilla.
- Add a handful of baby spinach or mixed greens over the hummus.
- Top with the roasted vegetables.
- If desired, sprinkle with crumbled feta cheese and sliced black olives.
- Garnish with fresh herbs if using.

4. **Wrap and Serve:**
   - Roll up the tortillas tightly to enclose the filling, folding in the sides as you go.
   - Slice the wraps in half diagonally for easier eating.
   - Serve immediately, or wrap in parchment paper or foil for a portable lunch.

Tips:

- **Vegetable Variations:** Feel free to use other vegetables such as mushrooms, asparagus, or carrots based on your preference or what's in season.
- **Hummus Flavors:** Experiment with different hummus flavors to match your taste. Spicy or herbed hummus can add a unique twist.
- **Make Ahead:** Roasted vegetables can be made in advance and stored in the refrigerator for up to 4 days, making this a convenient meal option.

Roasted Veggie and Hummus Wraps are a versatile and tasty meal option that combines the savory flavors of roasted vegetables with the creamy texture of hummus. These wraps are perfect for a healthy lunch, a quick dinner, or a nutritious snack!

Strawberry and Goat Cheese Bruschetta

Ingredients:

For the Bruschetta:

- 1 baguette or ciabatta loaf
- 4 ounces goat cheese, softened
- 1 tablespoon honey
- 1 tablespoon balsamic glaze (store-bought or homemade)
- 1 cup fresh strawberries, hulled and sliced
- 1 tablespoon fresh basil, thinly sliced (optional)
- 1 teaspoon finely chopped fresh mint (optional)
- Salt and freshly ground black pepper to taste

For Garnish:

- Fresh basil or mint leaves
- Extra honey for drizzling

Instructions:

1. **Prepare the Bread:**
   - Preheat your oven to 375°F (190°C).
   - Slice the baguette or ciabatta loaf into 1/2-inch thick slices.
   - Arrange the bread slices on a baking sheet in a single layer.
   - Toast the bread in the oven for 8-10 minutes, or until golden and crisp. Flip halfway through to ensure even toasting.
2. **Prepare the Goat Cheese Mixture:**
   - In a small bowl, mix the softened goat cheese with honey until smooth and well combined.
3. **Assemble the Bruschetta:**
   - Spread a generous layer of the honey-goat cheese mixture on each toasted bread slice.
   - Arrange the sliced strawberries on top of the goat cheese.
   - Drizzle with balsamic glaze.
   - Sprinkle with thinly sliced fresh basil and/or finely chopped mint if desired.
   - Season with a pinch of salt and freshly ground black pepper.
4. **Garnish and Serve:**
   - Garnish with additional fresh basil or mint leaves and a light drizzle of honey.
   - Serve immediately while the bread is still crisp.

Tips:

- **Balsamic Glaze:** If you don't have balsamic glaze, you can make it by reducing balsamic vinegar over medium heat until it thickens into a syrupy consistency. Allow it to cool before using.
- **Cheese Variations:** If you're not a fan of goat cheese, you can substitute with ricotta or cream cheese for a different flavor profile.
- **Additions:** For extra flavor, consider adding a sprinkle of toasted nuts like almonds or walnuts for crunch.

Strawberry and Goat Cheese Bruschetta is a delightful combination of sweet and savory flavors, perfect for impressing guests at a gathering or enjoying as a special appetizer. The contrast between the creamy goat cheese and fresh strawberries, along with the tangy balsamic glaze, creates a memorable and delicious bite!

Heart-Shaped Ravioli with Alfredo Sauce

Ingredients:

For the Heart-Shaped Ravioli:

- 12 ounces heart-shaped ravioli (store-bought or homemade)
- Salt, for pasta water
- 1 tablespoon olive oil (for tossing)

For the Alfredo Sauce:

- 4 tablespoons unsalted butter
- 1 cup heavy cream
- 1 cup grated Parmesan cheese
- 2 cloves garlic, minced
- 1/4 teaspoon nutmeg (optional)
- Salt and freshly ground black pepper, to taste
- Fresh parsley or basil, chopped (for garnish)

For Garnish:

- Extra grated Parmesan cheese
- Fresh parsley or basil leaves

Instructions:

1. **Cook the Ravioli:**
    - Bring a large pot of salted water to a boil.
    - Add the heart-shaped ravioli and cook according to the package instructions or until they float to the top and are tender (usually 2-4 minutes for fresh ravioli).
    - Drain the ravioli and toss gently with olive oil to prevent sticking.
2. **Prepare the Alfredo Sauce:**
    - In a medium saucepan, melt the butter over medium heat.
    - Add the minced garlic and cook for about 1 minute, or until fragrant but not browned.
    - Stir in the heavy cream and bring to a gentle simmer.
    - Reduce the heat to low and gradually add the grated Parmesan cheese, stirring constantly until the cheese is melted and the sauce is smooth.
    - Season with salt, freshly ground black pepper, and nutmeg (if using).
    - Continue to cook on low heat until the sauce thickens slightly, about 2-3 minutes.
3. **Combine Ravioli and Sauce:**
    - Gently toss the cooked ravioli with the Alfredo sauce until evenly coated.
4. **Serve:**
    - Transfer the ravioli with Alfredo sauce to serving plates or a large serving dish.
    - Garnish with extra grated Parmesan cheese and chopped fresh parsley or basil.

Tips:

- **Ravioli Options:** If you can't find heart-shaped ravioli, any shape will work, though heart-shaped adds a lovely touch for special occasions.
- **Homemade Ravioli:** If making homemade ravioli, ensure they are sealed well to prevent filling from leaking during cooking.
- **Cream Alternatives:** For a lighter sauce, you can use half-and-half instead of heavy cream, though the sauce may be less rich.

Heart-Shaped Ravioli with Alfredo Sauce is a delectable combination of tender ravioli and a creamy, cheesy sauce that is perfect for a romantic dinner or any special occasion. The heart-shaped ravioli adds a touch of charm, while the Alfredo sauce brings rich, comforting flavors to every bite. Enjoy this delightful dish with your loved ones or as a treat for yourself!

Bacon-Wrapped Stuffed Mushrooms

Ingredients:

For the Stuffed Mushrooms:

- 12 large white or cremini mushrooms (stems removed and cleaned)
- 4 ounces cream cheese, softened
- 1/4 cup grated Parmesan cheese
- 1/4 cup finely chopped cooked bacon (about 2-3 slices)
- 2 tablespoons chopped fresh parsley (or 1 tablespoon dried parsley)
- 1 clove garlic, minced
- Salt and freshly ground black pepper to taste
- 12 slices bacon (one per mushroom)

For Garnish:

- Extra chopped parsley
- Additional grated Parmesan cheese (optional)

Instructions:

1. **Prepare the Mushrooms:**
   - Preheat your oven to 375°F (190°C).
   - Clean the mushrooms and remove the stems. You can use a small spoon to gently scrape out any remaining gills if desired.
2. **Prepare the Filling:**
   - In a medium bowl, mix together the softened cream cheese, grated Parmesan cheese, chopped bacon, chopped parsley, minced garlic, salt, and black pepper until well combined.
3. **Stuff the Mushrooms:**
   - Spoon the cream cheese mixture into each mushroom cap, packing it in slightly to ensure it stays put.
4. **Wrap with Bacon:**
   - Cut the bacon slices in half if they are too long to wrap around the mushrooms.
   - Wrap each stuffed mushroom with a half slice of bacon, securing it with a toothpick if necessary. Make sure the bacon is wrapped tightly around the mushroom to ensure it cooks evenly.
5. **Bake:**
   - Place the bacon-wrapped mushrooms on a baking sheet lined with parchment paper or a wire rack.
   - Bake in the preheated oven for 20-25 minutes, or until the bacon is crispy and the stuffing is hot and bubbly. If needed, you can broil the mushrooms for the last 2-3 minutes to crisp up the bacon.
6. **Serve:**

- Remove the mushrooms from the oven and let them cool slightly.
- Garnish with additional chopped parsley and grated Parmesan cheese if desired.

Tips:

- **Bacon Variations:** For a different flavor, you can use flavored bacon (e.g., maple or peppered) or try turkey bacon for a lighter option.
- **Stuffing Options:** Feel free to experiment with other ingredients in the stuffing, such as chopped nuts, diced vegetables, or other types of cheese.
- **Make Ahead:** You can prepare the stuffed mushrooms in advance, wrap them with bacon, and refrigerate until ready to bake. Add a few extra minutes to the baking time if baking from cold.

Bacon-Wrapped Stuffed Mushrooms are a delightful combination of flavors and textures, with creamy cheese and crispy bacon creating a delicious bite. Perfect for any occasion, these appetizers are sure to be a hit at your next gathering!

Caprese Stuffed Avocados

Ingredients:

- 2 ripe avocados
- 1 cup cherry or grape tomatoes, halved
- 1/2 cup mini mozzarella balls (or diced fresh mozzarella)
- 1/4 cup fresh basil leaves, chopped (or torn)
- 1 tablespoon extra-virgin olive oil
- 1 tablespoon balsamic glaze or balsamic vinegar
- Salt and freshly ground black pepper to taste
- Optional: Red pepper flakes for a bit of heat

Instructions:

1. **Prepare the Avocados:**
    - Cut the avocados in half lengthwise and remove the pit.
    - Scoop out a bit of the flesh from the center of each half to create more space for the filling, but be careful not to scoop too much and compromise the stability of the avocado.
2. **Prepare the Caprese Filling:**
    - In a medium bowl, combine the cherry or grape tomatoes, mini mozzarella balls, and chopped fresh basil.
    - Drizzle with extra-virgin olive oil and balsamic glaze or balsamic vinegar.
    - Season with salt and freshly ground black pepper to taste. Toss gently to combine.
3. **Stuff the Avocados:**
    - Spoon the Caprese filling into the center of each avocado half, evenly distributing the tomatoes and mozzarella.
4. **Garnish and Serve:**
    - Drizzle a bit more balsamic glaze over the stuffed avocados if desired.
    - Sprinkle with red pepper flakes for a touch of heat if you like.
    - Garnish with additional fresh basil leaves.
5. **Serve Immediately:**
    - Serve the stuffed avocados immediately to enjoy their freshness. They can also be served chilled or at room temperature.

Tips:

- **Avocado Ripeness:** Make sure your avocados are ripe but not overly soft to avoid them becoming mushy when stuffed.
- **Tomato Alternatives:** If cherry tomatoes aren't available, you can use regular tomatoes, but make sure to dice them into small pieces.
- **Cheese Options:** If mini mozzarella balls are unavailable, you can use diced fresh mozzarella or even a sprinkle of crumbled feta cheese for a different twist.

Caprese Stuffed Avocados are a deliciously simple and elegant dish that brings together the creamy texture of avocado with the bright, fresh flavors of a Caprese salad. Perfect for a healthy snack or a sophisticated appetizer, this recipe is sure to be a hit with anyone who loves fresh and flavorful ingredients!

Spicy Chicken and Avocado Salad

Ingredients:

For the Spicy Chicken:

- 2 boneless, skinless chicken breasts
- 2 tablespoons olive oil
- 1 tablespoon smoked paprika
- 1 teaspoon ground cumin
- 1 teaspoon chili powder
- 1/2 teaspoon cayenne pepper (adjust to taste)
- 1/2 teaspoon garlic powder
- Salt and freshly ground black pepper to taste

For the Salad:

- 1 large ripe avocado, diced
- 4 cups mixed salad greens (such as lettuce, spinach, arugula)
- 1 cup cherry tomatoes, halved
- 1/2 red onion, thinly sliced
- 1/2 cucumber, sliced
- 1/4 cup crumbled feta cheese (optional)
- 1/4 cup fresh cilantro or parsley, chopped

For the Dressing:

- 3 tablespoons olive oil
- 2 tablespoons lime juice (about 1 lime)
- 1 tablespoon honey or agave nectar
- 1 teaspoon Dijon mustard
- 1 clove garlic, minced
- Salt and freshly ground black pepper to taste

Instructions:

1. **Prepare the Spicy Chicken:**
    - Preheat your grill or a skillet over medium-high heat.
    - Rub the chicken breasts with olive oil and season with smoked paprika, cumin, chili powder, cayenne pepper, garlic powder, salt, and black pepper.
    - Grill or cook the chicken for 6-7 minutes per side, or until the internal temperature reaches 165°F (74°C) and the chicken is cooked through.
    - Remove the chicken from the heat and let it rest for 5 minutes before slicing it into strips or cubes.
2. **Prepare the Salad Ingredients:**

- In a large salad bowl, combine the mixed salad greens, diced avocado, cherry tomatoes, red onion, and cucumber.
- If using, add crumbled feta cheese and chopped cilantro or parsley.
3. **Make the Dressing:**
    - In a small bowl or jar, whisk together the olive oil, lime juice, honey (or agave nectar), Dijon mustard, minced garlic, salt, and black pepper until well combined.
4. **Assemble the Salad:**
    - Add the sliced chicken to the salad bowl.
    - Drizzle the dressing over the salad and toss gently to combine all ingredients.
5. **Serve:**
    - Serve the salad immediately, or refrigerate for up to 1 hour before serving if preparing in advance.

Tips:

- **Chicken Variations:** For added flavor, you can marinate the chicken in the spice mixture for 30 minutes before cooking.
- **Avocado Tips:** To prevent the avocado from browning, add it to the salad just before serving.
- **Spice Level:** Adjust the amount of cayenne pepper and chili powder according to your spice preference.

Spicy Chicken and Avocado Salad is a flavorful and nutritious meal that offers a satisfying combination of spicy chicken, creamy avocado, and fresh vegetables. The zesty dressing ties everything together, making this salad a delicious choice for any occasion!

Sweet and Sour Meatball Skewers

Ingredients:

For the Meatballs:

- 1 pound ground beef or a mixture of beef and pork
- 1/2 cup breadcrumbs
- 1/4 cup grated Parmesan cheese
- 1/4 cup finely chopped onion
- 1/4 cup chopped fresh parsley or dried Italian seasoning
- 1 large egg
- 2 cloves garlic, minced
- Salt and freshly ground black pepper to taste

For the Sweet and Sour Sauce:

- 1/2 cup ketchup
- 1/4 cup rice vinegar
- 1/4 cup brown sugar
- 2 tablespoons soy sauce
- 1 tablespoon cornstarch
- 1 tablespoon water
- 1 teaspoon minced fresh ginger (optional)

For Assembly:

- Wooden or metal skewers (soaked in water if wooden)
- 1 cup pineapple chunks (optional, for grilling)
- 1 red bell pepper, cut into chunks (optional, for grilling)
- 1 green bell pepper, cut into chunks (optional, for grilling)

Instructions:

1. **Prepare the Meatballs:**
   - In a large bowl, combine the ground beef, breadcrumbs, Parmesan cheese, chopped onion, parsley or Italian seasoning, egg, minced garlic, salt, and black pepper.
   - Mix until just combined; be careful not to overmix.
   - Form the mixture into 1-inch meatballs and place them on a baking sheet.
2. **Cook the Meatballs:**
   - **Grilling Method:** Preheat your grill to medium-high heat. Thread the meatballs onto skewers (about 4-5 meatballs per skewer). Grill the meatballs for 10-12 minutes, turning occasionally, until they are cooked through and have a nice char.
   - **Baking Method:** Preheat your oven to 400°F (200°C). Place the meatballs on a baking sheet and bake for 15-20 minutes, or until they are cooked through.

3. **Prepare the Sweet and Sour Sauce:**
   - In a medium saucepan, combine ketchup, rice vinegar, brown sugar, soy sauce, and minced ginger (if using).
   - In a small bowl, mix cornstarch and water to create a slurry.
   - Bring the sauce to a simmer over medium heat, stirring occasionally.
   - Add the cornstarch slurry to the sauce and continue to cook, stirring until the sauce thickens, about 2-3 minutes. Remove from heat.
4. **Assemble the Skewers:**
   - If desired, you can thread pineapple chunks and bell pepper pieces onto the skewers along with the meatballs.
   - Brush the skewers with the sweet and sour sauce or serve the sauce on the side for dipping.
5. **Serve:**
   - Serve the meatball skewers immediately, drizzled with extra sauce or with a side of sauce for dipping.

Tips:

- **Meatball Variations:** You can use ground turkey or chicken for a lighter option, or add finely chopped vegetables to the meatball mixture for extra flavor and nutrition.
- **Sauce Variations:** Adjust the sweetness or tanginess of the sauce to your taste by adding more brown sugar or vinegar.
- **Side Suggestions:** Serve with steamed rice or noodles for a complete meal.

Sweet and Sour Meatball Skewers offer a delightful blend of sweet and tangy flavors with the satisfying texture of juicy meatballs. Whether grilled or baked, these skewers are sure to be a hit at your next gathering or as a delicious main course. Enjoy the burst of flavors and the fun presentation of this dish!

Herb-Crusted Salmon with Lemon Dill Sauce

Ingredients:

For the Herb-Crusted Salmon:

- 4 salmon fillets (6 oz each), skinless
- 1/2 cup panko breadcrumbs
- 1/4 cup grated Parmesan cheese
- 2 tablespoons fresh parsley, finely chopped
- 1 tablespoon fresh thyme, finely chopped (or 1 teaspoon dried thyme)
- 1 tablespoon fresh basil, finely chopped (or 1 teaspoon dried basil)
- 1 clove garlic, minced
- 2 tablespoons Dijon mustard
- 2 tablespoons olive oil
- Salt and freshly ground black pepper to taste

For the Lemon Dill Sauce:

- 1 cup sour cream or Greek yogurt
- 2 tablespoons mayonnaise
- 1 tablespoon lemon juice (about 1/2 lemon)
- 1 tablespoon fresh dill, chopped (or 1 teaspoon dried dill)
- 1 teaspoon Dijon mustard
- 1 clove garlic, minced
- Salt and freshly ground black pepper to taste

Instructions:

1. **Prepare the Herb-Crusted Salmon:**
   - Preheat your oven to 400°F (200°C).
   - In a small bowl, mix together the panko breadcrumbs, grated Parmesan cheese, parsley, thyme, basil, minced garlic, salt, and black pepper.
   - Place the salmon fillets on a baking sheet lined with parchment paper or lightly greased.
   - Brush each salmon fillet with Dijon mustard.
   - Press the herb and breadcrumb mixture onto the top of each fillet, patting it down gently to adhere.
   - Drizzle with olive oil.
2. **Bake the Salmon:**
   - Bake in the preheated oven for 12-15 minutes, or until the salmon is cooked through and flakes easily with a fork. The herb crust should be golden brown.
3. **Prepare the Lemon Dill Sauce:**
   - In a small bowl, combine the sour cream (or Greek yogurt), mayonnaise, lemon juice, chopped dill, Dijon mustard, minced garlic, salt, and black pepper.

- Mix until smooth and well combined.
4. **Serve:**
    - Transfer the baked salmon fillets to serving plates.
    - Spoon the lemon dill sauce over the top or serve it on the side for dipping.

Tips:

- **Salmon Freshness:** Choose fresh, high-quality salmon for the best flavor and texture. If using frozen salmon, thaw it in the refrigerator overnight before cooking.
- **Herb Variations:** Feel free to experiment with other fresh herbs, such as tarragon or chives, depending on your preference.
- **Sauce Variations:** For a lighter sauce, you can use plain Greek yogurt instead of sour cream, and adjust the lemon juice and dill to taste.

Herb-Crusted Salmon with Lemon Dill Sauce is a beautifully balanced dish that combines the rich flavor of salmon with a crunchy herb crust and a creamy, tangy sauce. It's perfect for impressing guests or enjoying a delightful meal at home.

Heart-Shaped Tomato and Basil Pesto Puffs

Ingredients:

- 1 sheet (or 1 package) puff pastry, thawed (preferably from the freezer section)
- 1/4 cup basil pesto (store-bought or homemade)
- 1/2 cup cherry or grape tomatoes, halved
- 1/2 cup shredded mozzarella cheese (or crumbled feta cheese)
- 1 egg, beaten (for egg wash)
- 1 tablespoon olive oil (optional, for brushing)
- Fresh basil leaves, for garnish (optional)
- Salt and freshly ground black pepper, to taste

Instructions:

1. **Prepare the Puff Pastry:**
    - Preheat your oven to 375°F (190°C).
    - Roll out the puff pastry sheet on a lightly floured surface to smooth out creases.
    - Use a heart-shaped cookie cutter (or any other preferred shape) to cut out shapes from the puff pastry. Arrange the shapes on a baking sheet lined with parchment paper.
2. **Assemble the Puffs:**
    - Spread a thin layer of basil pesto on each puff pastry shape.
    - Top with a few halved cherry tomatoes and a sprinkle of shredded mozzarella cheese.
    - Season with a bit of salt and freshly ground black pepper.
3. **Add the Egg Wash:**
    - Brush the edges of the puff pastry with the beaten egg to help it become golden and crisp during baking.
4. **Bake the Puffs:**
    - Bake in the preheated oven for 12-15 minutes, or until the puff pastry is golden brown and the cheese is melted and bubbly.
5. **Garnish and Serve:**
    - Remove from the oven and let cool slightly.
    - Garnish with fresh basil leaves if desired.
    - Serve warm or at room temperature.

Tips:

- **Pesto Variations:** You can use sun-dried tomato pesto or other flavored pestos for a different twist.
- **Tomato Options:** If cherry tomatoes are not available, you can use diced regular tomatoes or even roasted tomatoes for a richer flavor.
- **Cheese Options:** Experiment with different cheeses such as goat cheese or Parmesan for varied flavors.

Heart-Shaped Tomato and Basil Pesto Puffs are a delicious and visually appealing treat that combines the freshness of basil and tomato with the flaky goodness of puff pastry. Perfect for any occasion where you want to add a touch of elegance and flavor to your appetizer spread!

Honey Mustard Chicken and Apple Sandwiches

Ingredients:

For the Chicken:

- 2 boneless, skinless chicken breasts
- 2 tablespoons olive oil
- 2 tablespoons honey mustard (store-bought or homemade)
- 1 teaspoon dried thyme (or 1 tablespoon fresh thyme)
- Salt and freshly ground black pepper to taste

For the Sandwiches:

- 4 slices of your favorite bread (such as sourdough, ciabatta, or whole grain)
- 1 apple, thinly sliced (such as Honeycrisp, Fuji, or Gala)
- 4 tablespoons honey mustard (or more, to taste)
- 4-6 lettuce leaves (such as romaine or butter lettuce)
- 4 slices cheddar cheese or your preferred cheese (optional)
- 1 tablespoon olive oil or butter (for toasting the bread, optional)

Instructions:

1. **Prepare the Chicken:**
    - Preheat your grill or a skillet over medium-high heat.
    - Season the chicken breasts with salt, black pepper, and dried thyme.
    - Brush the chicken breasts with olive oil and spread a thin layer of honey mustard on both sides.
    - Grill or cook the chicken for 6-7 minutes per side, or until the internal temperature reaches 165°F (74°C) and the chicken is cooked through.
    - Remove the chicken from the heat and let it rest for 5 minutes before slicing it into strips or cubes.
2. **Prepare the Sandwich Ingredients:**
    - Toast the bread slices if desired. To do this, heat a skillet over medium heat, add a bit of olive oil or butter, and toast the bread until golden brown and crispy.
    - Thinly slice the apple.
3. **Assemble the Sandwiches:**
    - Spread honey mustard on one side of each slice of toasted bread.
    - Layer the lettuce leaves on the honey mustard side of two of the bread slices.
    - Add the sliced chicken on top of the lettuce.
    - Arrange apple slices over the chicken.
    - If using cheese, place a slice of cheddar or your preferred cheese on top of the apples.
    - Top with the remaining slices of bread, honey mustard side down.
4. **Serve:**

- Cut the sandwiches in half if desired and serve immediately.

Tips:

- **Chicken Options:** For a quicker option, you can use pre-cooked chicken or rotisserie chicken.
- **Apple Variations:** Choose an apple variety that is crisp and sweet to complement the honey mustard flavor.
- **Cheese Options:** Try other cheeses such as Swiss or provolone if you prefer different flavors.

Honey Mustard Chicken and Apple Sandwiches offer a delicious blend of flavors and textures, from the savory chicken and tangy honey mustard to the sweet, crisp apples. This easy-to-make sandwich is perfect for a quick lunch or a casual dinner, and it's sure to be a hit with anyone who enjoys a mix of savory and sweet!

Heart-Shaped Sweet Potato Fries

Ingredients:

- 2 large sweet potatoes, peeled
- 2 tablespoons olive oil
- 1 tablespoon cornstarch
- 1 teaspoon paprika
- 1/2 teaspoon garlic powder
- 1/2 teaspoon onion powder
- 1/2 teaspoon ground cumin
- 1/2 teaspoon dried thyme or rosemary (optional)
- Salt and freshly ground black pepper to taste
- Fresh parsley or chives for garnish (optional)

Instructions:

1. **Prepare the Sweet Potatoes:**
   - Preheat your oven to 425°F (220°C).
   - Peel the sweet potatoes and slice them into 1/4-inch thick planks. Use a heart-shaped cookie cutter to cut the planks into heart shapes. Arrange the heart-shaped sweet potatoes on a baking sheet lined with parchment paper.
2. **Season the Sweet Potatoes:**
   - In a large bowl, toss the heart-shaped sweet potato pieces with cornstarch until they are lightly coated. This helps them become extra crispy.
   - Drizzle the olive oil over the sweet potato pieces and toss to coat evenly.
   - In a small bowl, mix together paprika, garlic powder, onion powder, ground cumin, thyme or rosemary (if using), salt, and black pepper.
   - Sprinkle the seasoning mixture over the sweet potatoes and toss to coat evenly.
3. **Bake the Fries:**
   - Arrange the seasoned sweet potato hearts in a single layer on the baking sheet. Be sure not to overcrowd them to ensure they crisp up nicely.
   - Bake in the preheated oven for 20-25 minutes, flipping the fries halfway through, until they are golden brown and crispy on the edges.
4. **Serve:**
   - Remove from the oven and let the sweet potato fries cool slightly.
   - Garnish with fresh parsley or chives if desired.
   - Serve warm with your favorite dipping sauce or alongside your meal.

Tips:

- **Cutting Shapes:** For best results, use a sharp heart-shaped cookie cutter and cut the sweet potatoes while they are still firm. If the sweet potatoes are too soft, it will be difficult to cut them into shapes.

- **Crispiness:** Tossing the sweet potatoes with cornstarch helps to create a crispier texture. Make sure they are well-coated with oil and seasoning for even crisping.
- **Seasoning Variations:** Feel free to adjust the seasoning according to your taste or experiment with other spices like cayenne pepper for a bit of heat.

Heart-Shaped Sweet Potato Fries are a delightful and creative way to enjoy sweet potatoes. Their cute shape adds a special touch to your meal, making them perfect for festive occasions, special dinners, or just as a fun treat for the family!

Shrimp Scampi Linguine

Ingredients:

- 8 oz linguine (or any pasta of your choice)
- 1 lb large shrimp, peeled and deveined
- 3 tablespoons butter
- 3 tablespoons olive oil
- 4 cloves garlic, minced
- 1/4 teaspoon red pepper flakes (optional, for a bit of heat)
- 1/2 cup dry white wine (such as Sauvignon Blanc or Chardonnay) or chicken broth
- Juice of 1 lemon
- 1/4 cup chopped fresh parsley
- Salt and freshly ground black pepper, to taste
- 1/4 cup grated Parmesan cheese (optional, for serving)

Instructions:

1. **Cook the Linguine:**
   - Bring a large pot of salted water to a boil. Cook the linguine according to the package instructions until al dente. Reserve 1/2 cup of pasta cooking water, then drain the linguine and set aside.
2. **Prepare the Shrimp:**
   - While the pasta is cooking, heat 2 tablespoons of butter and 2 tablespoons of olive oil in a large skillet over medium-high heat.
   - Add the shrimp to the skillet in a single layer. Cook for 1-2 minutes on each side, or until the shrimp are pink and opaque. Remove the shrimp from the skillet and set aside.
3. **Make the Scampi Sauce:**
   - In the same skillet, add the remaining 1 tablespoon of butter and 1 tablespoon of olive oil.
   - Add the minced garlic and red pepper flakes (if using). Sauté for about 30 seconds, or until the garlic is fragrant but not browned.
   - Pour in the white wine (or chicken broth) and lemon juice. Bring to a simmer and cook for 2-3 minutes, allowing the sauce to reduce slightly.
4. **Combine Everything:**
   - Return the cooked shrimp to the skillet and toss to coat them in the sauce.
   - Add the cooked linguine to the skillet, tossing to combine and coat the pasta with the sauce. If the sauce seems too thick, add a bit of the reserved pasta cooking water until you reach the desired consistency.
5. **Finish and Serve:**
   - Stir in the chopped parsley and season with salt and black pepper to taste.
   - Remove from heat and serve immediately, garnished with grated Parmesan cheese if desired.

Tips:

- **Shrimp Size:** Use large shrimp for the best texture, but you can use smaller shrimp if preferred.
- **Wine Substitute:** If you prefer not to use wine, chicken broth works well as a substitute.
- **Pasta Water:** The reserved pasta water helps to emulsify the sauce and make it cling better to the pasta.

Shrimp Scampi Linguine is a delicious and sophisticated dish that's surprisingly easy to make. The combination of garlic, butter, and lemon creates a rich and flavorful sauce that complements the shrimp perfectly. This dish is perfect for a special dinner or a weeknight treat!

Warm Spinach and Artichoke Dip

Ingredients:

- 1 tablespoon olive oil
- 2 cloves garlic, minced
- 10 oz fresh spinach (or 1 package frozen chopped spinach, thawed and drained)
- 1 can (14 oz) artichoke hearts, drained and chopped
- 1/2 cup sour cream
- 1/2 cup mayonnaise
- 1 cup grated Parmesan cheese
- 1 cup shredded mozzarella cheese
- 1/2 teaspoon dried oregano
- 1/4 teaspoon dried thyme
- Salt and freshly ground black pepper to taste
- Optional: 1/4 teaspoon red pepper flakes (for a bit of heat)

Instructions:

1. **Prepare the Spinach:**
    - If using fresh spinach, heat the olive oil in a large skillet over medium heat. Add the minced garlic and sauté for 1 minute until fragrant.
    - Add the fresh spinach in batches, cooking until wilted and reduced in volume. Remove the spinach from the skillet and let it cool slightly, then squeeze out excess moisture and chop it roughly.
    - If using frozen spinach, make sure it is thoroughly thawed and well-drained before chopping.
2. **Combine the Ingredients:**
    - Preheat your oven to 375°F (190°C).
    - In a large bowl, combine the chopped spinach, artichoke hearts, sour cream, mayonnaise, grated Parmesan cheese, shredded mozzarella cheese, dried oregano, dried thyme, and salt and pepper.
    - Stir until all ingredients are well mixed. If using, add red pepper flakes for a bit of heat.
3. **Bake the Dip:**
    - Transfer the mixture to a baking dish (such as an 8-inch square dish or a small casserole dish).
    - Bake in the preheated oven for 20-25 minutes, or until the top is golden and bubbly.
4. **Serve:**
    - Remove from the oven and let the dip cool for a few minutes before serving.
    - Serve warm with your choice of dippers such as sliced baguette, crackers, tortilla chips, or fresh vegetable sticks.

Tips:

- **Cheese Variations:** You can experiment with other cheeses like cheddar or Gruyère for different flavors.
- **Make Ahead:** You can prepare the dip up to a day in advance. Store it in the refrigerator, then bake it just before serving.
- **Add-ins:** For extra flavor, consider adding chopped sun-dried tomatoes, bacon bits, or sautéed onions.

Warm Spinach and Artichoke Dip is a rich and creamy dish that is always a hit at gatherings. With its combination of cheesy goodness and hearty vegetables, it's perfect for sharing and will keep everyone coming back for more!

Grilled Veggie and Pesto Flatbread

Ingredients:

For the Flatbread:

- 2 store-bought or homemade flatbreads (or naan bread)
- 1/4 cup olive oil
- 1/2 cup pesto (store-bought or homemade)
- 1 cup shredded mozzarella cheese (or any cheese of your choice)

For the Grilled Vegetables:

- 1 red bell pepper, sliced
- 1 zucchini, sliced into rounds
- 1 yellow squash, sliced into rounds
- 1 red onion, sliced
- 1 tablespoon olive oil
- Salt and freshly ground black pepper to taste
- 1/2 teaspoon dried oregano or thyme (optional)

For Garnish:

- Fresh basil leaves, torn or chopped
- Balsamic glaze (optional, for drizzling)

Instructions:

1. **Prepare the Vegetables:**
    - Preheat your grill or grill pan to medium-high heat.
    - Toss the sliced bell pepper, zucchini, yellow squash, and red onion with olive oil, salt, black pepper, and dried oregano or thyme if using.
    - Grill the vegetables for about 3-4 minutes per side, or until they are tender and have nice grill marks. Remove from the grill and set aside.
2. **Prepare the Flatbreads:**
    - Preheat your oven to 400°F (200°C) if you're using it to crisp the flatbreads.
    - Brush each flatbread with olive oil on both sides. This helps them become crispy when baked.
    - Spread a thin layer of pesto over each flatbread, leaving a small border around the edges.
    - Sprinkle shredded mozzarella cheese evenly over the pesto.
3. **Assemble and Bake:**
    - Arrange the grilled vegetables evenly over the cheese on the flatbreads.
    - Place the flatbreads on a baking sheet and bake in the preheated oven for about 10-12 minutes, or until the cheese is melted and bubbly and the flatbreads are crispy.

4. **Garnish and Serve:**
   - Remove the flatbreads from the oven and let them cool slightly.
   - Garnish with fresh basil leaves and a drizzle of balsamic glaze if desired.
   - Slice into pieces and serve warm.

Tips:

- **Pesto Variations:** You can use different types of pesto, such as sun-dried tomato pesto or spinach pesto, for a unique flavor.
- **Cheese Options:** Feel free to experiment with different cheeses like goat cheese, feta, or provolone.
- **Veggie Choices:** Customize the grilled vegetables based on what's in season or your personal preferences. Mushrooms, cherry tomatoes, and eggplant are also great options.

Grilled Veggie and Pesto Flatbread is a versatile and flavorful dish that pairs well with a side salad or can be enjoyed on its own. The combination of grilled veggies and pesto on a crispy flatbread makes for a satisfying and delicious meal that's easy to prepare and perfect for any occasion!

Creamy Butternut Squash Soup

Ingredients:

- 1 large butternut squash (about 3-4 lbs), peeled, seeded, and cubed
- 2 tablespoons olive oil
- 1 large onion, chopped
- 2 cloves garlic, minced
- 1 large carrot, peeled and chopped
- 1 celery stalk, chopped
- 4 cups vegetable or chicken broth
- 1/2 cup heavy cream (or coconut milk for a dairy-free option)
- 1/2 teaspoon ground cumin
- 1/2 teaspoon ground nutmeg
- 1/4 teaspoon ground cinnamon (optional)
- Salt and freshly ground black pepper to taste
- 2 tablespoons fresh parsley or chives, chopped (for garnish)
- Optional: 1-2 tablespoons maple syrup or honey (for added sweetness)

Instructions:

1. **Prepare the Squash:**
   - Preheat your oven to 400°F (200°C).
   - Arrange the cubed butternut squash on a baking sheet. Drizzle with 1 tablespoon of olive oil and season with salt and pepper. Toss to coat evenly.
   - Roast in the preheated oven for 25-30 minutes, or until the squash is tender and caramelized. Remove from the oven and set aside.
2. **Cook the Vegetables:**
   - In a large pot or Dutch oven, heat the remaining 1 tablespoon of olive oil over medium heat.
   - Add the chopped onion, garlic, carrot, and celery. Sauté for 5-7 minutes, or until the vegetables are softened and the onion is translucent.
3. **Combine and Simmer:**
   - Add the roasted butternut squash to the pot with the sautéed vegetables.
   - Pour in the vegetable or chicken broth, and bring the mixture to a boil. Reduce heat and let it simmer for 10 minutes, allowing the flavors to meld.
4. **Blend the Soup:**
   - Use an immersion blender to carefully blend the soup until smooth. Alternatively, you can transfer the soup in batches to a blender. Be cautious with hot liquids and blend in small batches if using a regular blender.
5. **Add Cream and Seasonings:**
   - Stir in the heavy cream (or coconut milk) and season with ground cumin, nutmeg, and cinnamon if using. Taste and adjust seasoning with salt and pepper. If you prefer a sweeter soup, add a bit of maple syrup or honey.
6. **Serve:**

- Ladle the soup into bowls and garnish with chopped fresh parsley or chives.
- Serve hot, with crusty bread or a side salad if desired.

Tips:

- **Roasting the Squash:** Roasting the squash brings out its natural sweetness and adds a deeper flavor to the soup. Ensure the cubes are evenly spaced on the baking sheet for even roasting.
- **Texture:** For a richer texture, you can add more cream or use full-fat coconut milk.
- **Flavor Variations:** Experiment with different spices like ginger or paprika to add additional layers of flavor.

Creamy Butternut Squash Soup is a rich and satisfying dish that's perfect for fall and winter. Its smooth, creamy texture and subtle sweetness make it a comforting and elegant choice for any meal. Enjoy this soup as a hearty lunch or as a delightful starter for a dinner party!

Heart-Shaped Pancetta and Egg Breakfast Sandwiches

Ingredients:

- 4 slices of your favorite bread (such as sourdough, ciabatta, or whole grain)
- 4 slices of pancetta (or bacon if pancetta is unavailable)
- 4 large eggs
- 2 tablespoons butter or olive oil
- 2 slices of cheese (optional, such as cheddar, Swiss, or American)
- Salt and freshly ground black pepper to taste
- Fresh herbs (optional, such as chives or parsley), chopped
- Heart-shaped cookie cutter
- Optional: avocado slices, tomato slices, or greens for added toppings

Instructions:

1. **Prepare the Bread:**
   - Use a heart-shaped cookie cutter to cut the bread slices into heart shapes. You can also use a knife to cut out heart shapes if you don't have a cookie cutter.
2. **Cook the Pancetta:**
   - Heat a skillet over medium heat. Add the pancetta slices and cook until crispy, about 2-3 minutes per side. Remove from the skillet and place on a paper towel to drain excess fat. Set aside.
3. **Cook the Eggs:**
   - In the same skillet, remove excess fat, leaving about 1 tablespoon. If needed, add a small amount of butter or oil to the skillet.
   - Crack each egg into the skillet, cooking to your preferred doneness (sunny-side up, over-easy, or scrambled). Season with salt and pepper to taste. If using cheese, place a slice on top of the egg during the last minute of cooking to let it melt slightly.
4. **Toast the Bread:**
   - In a separate pan, toast the heart-shaped bread slices until golden brown and crispy. You can also do this in a toaster or under a broiler.
5. **Assemble the Sandwiches:**
   - Spread a small amount of butter or additional toppings on the toasted bread if desired.
   - Place a slice of crispy pancetta on one slice of bread.
   - Top with a cooked egg. Add any additional toppings such as avocado slices, tomato slices, or greens if using.
   - Place the second slice of bread on top, pressing down gently.
6. **Serve:**
   - Garnish with fresh herbs if desired and serve immediately while warm.

Tips:

- **Cheese Options:** Customize the sandwiches with different cheeses or omit the cheese for a lighter option.
- **Toppings:** Feel free to add other breakfast favorites like sautéed mushrooms, caramelized onions, or a spread of avocado or aioli.
- **Egg Variations:** Adjust the egg cooking method to suit your taste, such as poached or fried.

Heart-Shaped Pancetta and Egg Breakfast Sandwiches are a delightful way to add a touch of whimsy and flavor to your breakfast. They're perfect for special occasions like Valentine's Day or simply to make your morning routine a bit more enjoyable. Enjoy these heartwarming sandwiches with a side of fruit or a fresh green salad for a complete meal!

Pear and Blue Cheese Salad

Ingredients:

- 4 cups mixed greens (such as arugula, spinach, and/or baby kale)
- 2 ripe pears, cored and thinly sliced
- 1/2 cup crumbled blue cheese
- 1/4 cup walnuts or pecans, toasted and roughly chopped
- 1/4 cup dried cranberries or pomegranate seeds (optional, for a touch of sweetness)
- 1/4 cup thinly sliced red onion (optional)
- Freshly ground black pepper to taste

For the Dressing:

- 1/4 cup extra-virgin olive oil
- 2 tablespoons balsamic vinegar (or apple cider vinegar)
- 1 tablespoon honey or maple syrup
- 1 teaspoon Dijon mustard
- Salt to taste

Instructions:

1. **Prepare the Dressing:**
    - In a small bowl or jar, whisk together the olive oil, balsamic vinegar, honey (or maple syrup), Dijon mustard, and a pinch of salt until well combined. Adjust the seasoning to taste and set aside.
2. **Toast the Nuts:**
    - In a dry skillet over medium heat, toast the walnuts or pecans until they are fragrant and lightly browned, about 3-5 minutes. Stir frequently to prevent burning. Let them cool before adding to the salad.
3. **Assemble the Salad:**
    - In a large salad bowl, toss the mixed greens with a small amount of the prepared dressing, just enough to lightly coat the leaves.
    - Arrange the sliced pears on top of the greens.
    - Sprinkle the crumbled blue cheese, toasted nuts, and dried cranberries (if using) over the salad.
    - Add the thinly sliced red onion if desired.
4. **Serve:**
    - Drizzle the remaining dressing over the salad or serve it on the side.
    - Season with freshly ground black pepper to taste.
    - Toss gently to combine all ingredients just before serving.

Tips:

- **Pear Varieties:** Use ripe but firm pears such as Bosc, Anjou, or Bartlett for the best texture and flavor.
- **Cheese Alternatives:** If you're not a fan of blue cheese, try substituting with feta or goat cheese.
- **Add Protein:** For a more substantial meal, add grilled chicken, steak, or tofu.

Pear and Blue Cheese Salad offers a wonderful balance of flavors and textures, from the creamy and tangy blue cheese to the sweet and juicy pears. The crunchy nuts and a hint of sweetness from dried fruit or pomegranate seeds make this salad a delightful addition to any meal. Enjoy this elegant and refreshing salad as a perfect complement to any occasion!

Heart-Shaped Cornbread Muffins

Ingredients:

- 1 cup cornmeal
- 1 cup all-purpose flour
- 1/4 cup granulated sugar
- 1 tablespoon baking powder
- 1/2 teaspoon salt
- 1 cup milk (whole or 2%)
- 1/4 cup vegetable oil or melted butter
- 2 large eggs
- 1 cup fresh or frozen corn kernels (optional, for added texture)
- 1/2 cup shredded cheddar cheese (optional, for a cheesy version)

Instructions:

1. **Preheat the Oven:**
   - Preheat your oven to 400°F (200°C). Grease a heart-shaped muffin tin or line it with paper liners.
2. **Prepare the Dry Ingredients:**
   - In a large bowl, whisk together the cornmeal, flour, sugar, baking powder, and salt until well combined.
3. **Mix the Wet Ingredients:**
   - In another bowl, whisk together the milk, vegetable oil (or melted butter), and eggs until smooth and well blended.
4. **Combine the Ingredients:**
   - Pour the wet ingredients into the dry ingredients. Stir gently until just combined. Avoid overmixing, as this can make the cornbread muffins dense.
   - If using, fold in the corn kernels and shredded cheddar cheese.
5. **Fill the Muffin Tin:**
   - Spoon the batter into the prepared heart-shaped muffin tin, filling each cup about 2/3 full.
6. **Bake:**
   - Bake in the preheated oven for 15-18 minutes, or until the tops are golden brown and a toothpick inserted into the center comes out clean.
7. **Cool:**
   - Allow the muffins to cool in the pan for a few minutes before transferring them to a wire rack to cool completely.
8. **Serve:**
   - Serve warm or at room temperature. These heart-shaped cornbread muffins are great on their own or with a bit of butter and honey.

Tips:

- **Corn Kernels:** If using frozen corn kernels, make sure to thaw and drain them before adding to the batter.
- **Cheese:** For an extra flavor boost, try adding some crumbled bacon or finely chopped jalapeños for a spicy kick.
- **Storage:** Store leftover muffins in an airtight container at room temperature for up to 3 days, or freeze for up to 3 months.

Heart-Shaped Cornbread Muffins are a delightful and playful way to enjoy a traditional cornbread recipe. Their tender, moist texture and slightly sweet flavor make them a perfect side dish for soups, stews, or just a simple snack. Whether you're celebrating a special occasion or simply want to add a bit of fun to your baking, these muffins are sure to bring a smile to your face!

Spaghetti with Garlic and Olive Oil

Ingredients:

- 12 oz (340 g) spaghetti
- 1/2 cup extra-virgin olive oil
- 6 cloves garlic, thinly sliced
- 1/2 teaspoon red pepper flakes (adjust to taste for spiciness)
- 1/2 cup fresh parsley, chopped
- Salt to taste
- Freshly ground black pepper to taste
- Grated Parmesan cheese (optional, for serving)
- Lemon zest (optional, for garnish)

Instructions:

1. **Cook the Spaghetti:**
    - Bring a large pot of salted water to a boil. Add the spaghetti and cook according to the package instructions until al dente.
    - Reserve 1 cup of pasta cooking water, then drain the pasta.
2. **Prepare the Garlic and Olive Oil:**
    - While the pasta is cooking, heat the olive oil in a large skillet over medium heat.
    - Add the sliced garlic and cook, stirring frequently, until the garlic is golden brown and fragrant but not burned, about 2-3 minutes. Be careful not to let the garlic burn, as it can become bitter.
3. **Combine Pasta and Garlic Oil:**
    - Add the red pepper flakes to the garlic and olive oil mixture.
    - Add the drained spaghetti to the skillet, tossing to coat the pasta with the garlic oil. If the pasta seems dry, gradually add some of the reserved pasta cooking water until you reach the desired consistency.
4. **Add Finishing Touches:**
    - Stir in the chopped parsley and season with salt and freshly ground black pepper to taste.
    - Toss everything together until well combined and heated through.
5. **Serve:**
    - Serve the spaghetti hot, garnished with additional parsley, grated Parmesan cheese, and a sprinkle of lemon zest if desired.

Tips:

- **Garlic Slicing:** Thinly slice the garlic to ensure it cooks evenly and releases its flavor into the oil.
- **Pasta Water:** The reserved pasta cooking water helps to create a silky sauce that clings to the pasta. Add it gradually to avoid making the dish too watery.

- **Variations:** Feel free to add extras like sautéed mushrooms, cherry tomatoes, or olives for additional flavor and texture.

Spaghetti with Garlic and Olive Oil is a testament to the simplicity and elegance of Italian cuisine. Its rich, savory flavors and satisfying texture make it a favorite among pasta lovers. This dish is perfect for a quick weeknight meal or a light yet flavorful lunch or dinner. Enjoy the taste of Italy with this delicious and easy-to-make recipe!

Balsamic Glazed Brussels Sprouts

Ingredients:

- 1 1/2 lbs (680 g) Brussels sprouts, trimmed and halved
- 2 tablespoons olive oil
- Salt and freshly ground black pepper to taste
- 1/4 cup balsamic vinegar
- 2 tablespoons honey or maple syrup
- 1/4 cup chopped nuts (such as almonds or walnuts) or crispy bacon (optional, for added texture)
- 1/4 cup grated Parmesan cheese (optional, for serving)
- Fresh parsley, chopped (optional, for garnish)

Instructions:

1. **Prepare the Brussels Sprouts:**
   - Preheat your oven to 400°F (200°C).
   - Trim the ends of the Brussels sprouts and cut them in half. If any of the outer leaves fall off, you can discard them or use them in the dish.
2. **Season and Roast:**
   - In a large bowl, toss the halved Brussels sprouts with olive oil, salt, and black pepper until they are evenly coated.
   - Spread the Brussels sprouts out in a single layer on a baking sheet. Make sure they are not crowded to ensure they roast evenly.
   - Roast in the preheated oven for 20-25 minutes, or until the Brussels sprouts are tender and golden brown, tossing halfway through for even roasting.
3. **Prepare the Balsamic Glaze:**
   - While the Brussels sprouts are roasting, prepare the balsamic glaze.
   - In a small saucepan, combine the balsamic vinegar and honey (or maple syrup). Bring to a simmer over medium heat.
   - Reduce the heat and let the mixture simmer for about 5-7 minutes, or until it has thickened slightly and reduced by about half. Stir occasionally to prevent burning. Remove from heat and set aside.
4. **Toss and Serve:**
   - Once the Brussels sprouts are done roasting, transfer them to a serving bowl.
   - Drizzle the balsamic glaze over the Brussels sprouts and toss to coat evenly.
   - If using, sprinkle with chopped nuts or crispy bacon for added texture.
   - Garnish with grated Parmesan cheese and fresh parsley, if desired.

Tips:

- **Even Roasting:** To ensure the Brussels sprouts roast evenly and get crispy, make sure they are spread out in a single layer on the baking sheet.

- **Glaze Consistency:** The balsamic glaze should be thick but still pourable. If it gets too thick, you can thin it out with a splash of water.
- **Flavor Variations:** Add a sprinkle of red pepper flakes for a bit of heat or a squeeze of lemon juice for a fresh contrast.

Balsamic Glazed Brussels Sprouts are a perfect side dish for holiday meals, weeknight dinners, or any time you want to enjoy a flavorful and healthy vegetable dish. The combination of the caramelized Brussels sprouts with the sweet and tangy balsamic glaze makes this recipe a crowd-pleaser that's both elegant and easy to prepare. Enjoy!

Roasted Red Pepper and Spinach Frittata

Ingredients:

- 1 tablespoon olive oil
- 1 small onion, diced
- 1 red bell pepper, roasted, peeled, and chopped (or use jarred roasted red peppers)
- 2 cups fresh spinach, roughly chopped
- 6 large eggs
- 1/4 cup milk (whole, 2%, or a dairy-free alternative)
- 1/2 cup shredded cheese (such as feta, goat cheese, or cheddar)
- Salt and freshly ground black pepper to taste
- 1/4 teaspoon dried oregano or basil (optional)
- Fresh herbs for garnish (optional, such as parsley or chives)

Instructions:

1. **Prepare the Oven and Pan:**
    - Preheat your oven to 375°F (190°C).
    - Heat an oven-safe skillet (preferably cast iron or a non-stick skillet) over medium heat.
2. **Cook the Vegetables:**
    - Add the olive oil to the skillet. Once hot, add the diced onion and cook until softened and translucent, about 4-5 minutes.
    - Add the chopped roasted red pepper and cook for another 2 minutes.
    - Stir in the spinach and cook until wilted, about 1-2 minutes. Season with a pinch of salt and pepper.
3. **Prepare the Egg Mixture:**
    - In a bowl, whisk together the eggs, milk, and a bit more salt and pepper. Add the shredded cheese and mix until well combined.
4. **Combine and Cook:**
    - Pour the egg mixture over the cooked vegetables in the skillet. Stir gently to distribute the vegetables evenly throughout the eggs.
    - Cook on the stovetop for about 2-3 minutes, or until the edges start to set.
5. **Bake:**
    - Transfer the skillet to the preheated oven. Bake for 15-20 minutes, or until the frittata is fully set in the center and the top is golden brown. You can check for doneness by inserting a toothpick into the center—if it comes out clean, the frittata is done.
6. **Cool and Serve:**
    - Allow the frittata to cool slightly before slicing. Garnish with fresh herbs if desired.
    - Serve warm or at room temperature.

Tips:

- **Roasted Red Peppers:** If you're using jarred roasted red peppers, be sure to drain them well and pat them dry with a paper towel to avoid excess moisture.
- **Cheese:** Feel free to experiment with different cheeses based on your preference. Goat cheese or feta adds a tangy flavor, while cheddar or mozzarella will make it more creamy.
- **Make-Ahead:** This frittata can be made ahead of time and stored in the refrigerator for up to 3 days. It can be eaten cold or reheated in the oven.

Roasted Red Pepper and Spinach Frittata is a delicious and nutritious option that's as versatile as it is tasty. It's a great way to use up vegetables and can be adapted with whatever ingredients you have on hand. Enjoy this frittata for a satisfying and wholesome meal!

Spicy Tuna Stuffed Avocados

Ingredients:

- 2 ripe avocados
- 1 can (5 oz) tuna, drained (preferably in water)
- 2 tablespoons mayonnaise (or Greek yogurt for a lighter option)
- 1 tablespoon sriracha or hot sauce (adjust to taste)
- 1 tablespoon soy sauce
- 1 teaspoon lime juice
- 1 celery stalk, finely diced
- 1/4 cup red bell pepper, finely diced
- 1 tablespoon fresh cilantro, chopped (optional)
- Salt and freshly ground black pepper to taste
- Sesame seeds or chopped green onions for garnish (optional)

Instructions:

1. **Prepare the Avocados:**
   - Cut the avocados in half lengthwise and remove the pits. Scoop out a small amount of flesh from each half to create a little extra space for the filling. You can use the scooped-out avocado flesh in the tuna mixture or save it for another use.
2. **Make the Spicy Tuna Filling:**
   - In a medium bowl, combine the drained tuna, mayonnaise (or Greek yogurt), sriracha (or hot sauce), soy sauce, and lime juice. Mix well until everything is evenly incorporated.
   - Fold in the finely diced celery and red bell pepper. Add chopped cilantro if using. Season with salt and black pepper to taste.
3. **Stuff the Avocados:**
   - Spoon the spicy tuna mixture into the hollowed-out avocado halves, filling them generously.
4. **Garnish and Serve:**
   - Garnish with sesame seeds or chopped green onions if desired.
   - Serve immediately, or chill in the refrigerator for up to an hour before serving.

Tips:

- **Adjusting Spice Level:** You can adjust the amount of sriracha or hot sauce according to your taste preference. If you prefer a milder version, start with a smaller amount and add more as needed.
- **Freshness:** Use ripe avocados that are firm but slightly soft to the touch. Overripe avocados can become mushy.
- **Variations:** Add other ingredients to the tuna mixture like diced cucumber, olives, or a splash of lemon juice for additional flavors.

Spicy Tuna Stuffed Avocados offer a delightful balance of creamy and spicy flavors, making them a satisfying and healthy meal option. They're not only visually appealing but also packed with protein and healthy fats. Enjoy this easy-to-make dish as a nutritious and flavorful addition to your meal rotation!

Heart-Shaped Savory Scones

Ingredients:

- 2 1/4 cups all-purpose flour
- 1 tablespoon baking powder
- 1/2 teaspoon salt
- 1/2 teaspoon black pepper
- 1/2 teaspoon dried thyme or rosemary (or a mix of herbs)
- 1/2 cup (1 stick) cold unsalted butter, cut into small cubes
- 1 cup shredded cheese (cheddar, Gruyère, or your favorite cheese)
- 3/4 cup milk (whole or 2%)
- 1 large egg
- 2 tablespoons chopped fresh chives or parsley (optional, for extra flavor)
- 1 tablespoon milk (for brushing)
- Coarse sea salt or additional shredded cheese (optional, for topping)

Instructions:

1. **Preheat the Oven:**
   - Preheat your oven to 400°F (200°C). Line a baking sheet with parchment paper or lightly grease it.
2. **Prepare the Dry Ingredients:**
   - In a large bowl, whisk together the flour, baking powder, salt, black pepper, and dried thyme or rosemary.
3. **Cut in the Butter:**
   - Add the cold butter cubes to the flour mixture. Use a pastry cutter, fork, or your fingers to cut the butter into the flour until the mixture resembles coarse crumbs with pea-sized pieces of butter.
4. **Add Cheese and Herbs:**
   - Gently fold in the shredded cheese and chopped fresh chives or parsley if using.
5. **Mix the Wet Ingredients:**
   - In a separate bowl, whisk together the milk and egg until well combined.
6. **Combine and Form the Dough:**
   - Pour the wet ingredients into the dry ingredients and mix until just combined. The dough will be somewhat sticky but should hold together. Avoid over-mixing.
7. **Roll Out and Cut:**
   - Turn the dough onto a lightly floured surface. Pat or roll out the dough to about 1-inch thickness.
   - Use a heart-shaped cookie cutter to cut out scones. Gather the scraps, re-roll, and cut out remaining scones.
8. **Brush and Bake:**
   - Place the scones on the prepared baking sheet. Brush the tops with a tablespoon of milk and sprinkle with coarse sea salt or additional shredded cheese if desired.

- Bake for 15-20 minutes, or until the scones are golden brown and a toothpick inserted into the center comes out clean.
9. **Cool and Serve:**
    - Allow the scones to cool slightly on a wire rack before serving. Enjoy warm or at room temperature.

Tips:

- **Butter Temperature:** Ensure the butter is cold to achieve the best flaky texture in the scones.
- **Cheese Choices:** Experiment with different cheeses like feta or blue cheese for varied flavors.
- **Herbs:** Fresh herbs can be substituted for dried herbs if preferred.

Heart-Shaped Savory Scones are a delightful and versatile addition to any meal. Their tender crumb and savory flavor make them perfect for pairing with soups, salads, or even as a stand-alone treat. The heart shape adds a special touch, making these scones ideal for gatherings, celebrations, or just a fun baking project. Enjoy!

Chicken and Waffle Sliders

Ingredients:

For the Chicken:

- 1 lb (450 g) chicken tenders or boneless, skinless chicken breasts, cut into strips
- 1 cup buttermilk
- 1 cup all-purpose flour
- 1/2 cup cornstarch
- 1 teaspoon paprika
- 1 teaspoon garlic powder
- 1 teaspoon onion powder
- 1/2 teaspoon cayenne pepper (optional, for extra heat)
- Salt and freshly ground black pepper to taste
- Vegetable oil, for frying

For the Waffles:

- 1 1/2 cups all-purpose flour
- 2 tablespoons sugar
- 1 tablespoon baking powder
- 1/2 teaspoon salt
- 1 cup milk
- 1/4 cup vegetable oil
- 1 large egg
- 1 teaspoon vanilla extract

For Serving:

- Maple syrup or honey, for drizzling
- Pickles (optional)
- Lettuce or coleslaw (optional, for extra crunch)

Instructions:

1. **Prepare the Chicken:**
    - In a bowl, marinate the chicken strips in buttermilk for at least 30 minutes, or overnight for best results.
    - In a separate bowl, combine the flour, cornstarch, paprika, garlic powder, onion powder, cayenne pepper (if using), salt, and pepper.
    - Heat vegetable oil in a deep skillet or fryer to 350°F (175°C).
    - Remove chicken from the buttermilk and dredge each piece in the flour mixture, pressing lightly to adhere.

- Fry the chicken in batches until golden brown and crispy, about 4-5 minutes per batch. Ensure the chicken reaches an internal temperature of 165°F (74°C). Drain on paper towels.

2. **Make the Waffles:**
   - Preheat your waffle iron according to the manufacturer's instructions.
   - In a large bowl, whisk together the flour, sugar, baking powder, and salt.
   - In another bowl, combine the milk, vegetable oil, egg, and vanilla extract.
   - Pour the wet ingredients into the dry ingredients and stir until just combined.
   - Cook the batter in the preheated waffle iron according to the manufacturer's instructions until golden brown and crisp. Allow waffles to cool slightly before cutting into smaller slider-sized pieces.

3. **Assemble the Sliders:**
   - Place a piece of fried chicken on one half of each waffle piece.
   - Drizzle with maple syrup or honey if desired.
   - Add pickles, lettuce, or coleslaw if using.
   - Top with the other half of the waffle to form a slider.

4. **Serve:**
   - Arrange the sliders on a platter and serve immediately while the waffles and chicken are still warm.

Tips:

- **Waffle Size:** For smaller sliders, cut waffles into quarters or use a mini waffle maker.
- **Chicken Coating:** For extra crunch, double-dip the chicken by first dredging in flour, then dipping in buttermilk, and dredging in flour again.
- **Make-Ahead:** Prepare the chicken and waffles ahead of time and reheat before assembling to save time.

Chicken and Waffle Sliders bring together the best of both worlds with their crispy chicken and fluffy waffles. This recipe is sure to be a hit at any gathering or special occasion, offering a delightful balance of flavors and textures in every bite. Enjoy!

Thai Peanut Chicken Salad

Ingredients:

For the Salad:

- 2 cups cooked chicken breast, shredded or sliced (grilled, baked, or rotisserie chicken works well)
- 4 cups mixed greens (such as romaine, spinach, or baby kale)
- 1 cup shredded cabbage (green or red)
- 1 cup shredded carrots
- 1/2 cup red bell pepper, thinly sliced
- 1/2 cup cucumber, thinly sliced
- 1/4 cup chopped fresh cilantro
- 1/4 cup chopped fresh basil (optional)
- 1/4 cup chopped peanuts (for garnish)
- Lime wedges (for serving)

For the Thai Peanut Dressing:

- 1/4 cup creamy peanut butter
- 2 tablespoons soy sauce or tamari
- 2 tablespoons rice vinegar
- 1 tablespoon honey or maple syrup
- 1 tablespoon sesame oil
- 1 clove garlic, minced
- 1 teaspoon fresh ginger, grated
- 1-2 tablespoons water (to thin the dressing, as needed)
- Red pepper flakes (optional, for added heat)

Instructions:

1. **Prepare the Dressing:**
    - In a small bowl or blender, whisk together the peanut butter, soy sauce, rice vinegar, honey, sesame oil, minced garlic, and grated ginger.
    - Add water, a tablespoon at a time, until you reach your desired consistency. The dressing should be creamy but pourable.
    - Adjust seasoning with red pepper flakes for heat, if desired.
2. **Assemble the Salad:**
    - In a large bowl, combine the mixed greens, shredded cabbage, shredded carrots, red bell pepper, and cucumber.
    - Add the cooked chicken on top of the vegetables.
3. **Dress and Toss:**
    - Drizzle the Thai peanut dressing over the salad.

- Toss gently to combine, ensuring all ingredients are well-coated with the dressing.
4. **Garnish and Serve:**
    - Sprinkle chopped peanuts, fresh cilantro, and basil over the top.
    - Serve the salad with lime wedges on the side for an extra burst of freshness.

Tips:

- **Chicken:** You can use leftover chicken or prepare it fresh. Grilling or baking the chicken with a bit of seasoning will add extra flavor.
- **Crunch:** For added crunch, consider adding crispy chow mein noodles or additional chopped peanuts.
- **Veggies:** Feel free to mix and match vegetables based on your preference or what you have on hand.

Thai Peanut Chicken Salad is a delightful and nutritious option that pairs well with a variety of cuisines and occasions. The combination of savory, sweet, and tangy flavors in the peanut dressing complements the freshness of the vegetables and the protein of the chicken, making it a satisfying and balanced meal. Enjoy this vibrant and tasty salad!

Mini Heart-Shaped Calzones

Ingredients:

For the Dough:

- 2 1/4 teaspoons (1 packet) active dry yeast
- 1 1/2 cups warm water (110°F/45°C)
- 1 tablespoon sugar
- 3 1/2 to 4 cups all-purpose flour
- 2 tablespoons olive oil
- 1 teaspoon salt

For the Filling:

- 1 cup ricotta cheese
- 1 cup shredded mozzarella cheese
- 1/2 cup grated Parmesan cheese
- 1/2 cup sliced pepperoni or cooked sausage (optional)
- 1/2 cup finely chopped cooked vegetables (such as bell peppers, mushrooms, or spinach)
- 1/2 teaspoon dried oregano or Italian seasoning
- 1/4 teaspoon garlic powder
- Salt and freshly ground black pepper to taste

For Assembly:

- 1 egg, beaten (for egg wash)
- Marinara sauce or pizza sauce, for dipping

Instructions:

1. **Prepare the Dough:**
    - In a small bowl, dissolve the sugar in warm water and sprinkle the yeast on top. Let it sit for about 5-10 minutes, or until the mixture is frothy.
    - In a large bowl, combine 3 1/2 cups of flour and salt. Make a well in the center and pour in the yeast mixture and olive oil.
    - Mix until the dough starts to come together, then turn it out onto a floured surface. Knead the dough for about 5-7 minutes, adding additional flour if necessary, until the dough is smooth and elastic.
    - Place the dough in a lightly oiled bowl, cover with a damp cloth, and let it rise in a warm place for about 1-2 hours, or until doubled in size.
2. **Prepare the Filling:**
    - In a bowl, combine the ricotta cheese, mozzarella cheese, Parmesan cheese, and optional fillings like pepperoni or vegetables.
    - Season with oregano, garlic powder, salt, and pepper. Mix well.

3. **Shape the Calzones:**
    - Preheat your oven to 375°F (190°C). Line a baking sheet with parchment paper.
    - Punch down the risen dough and turn it out onto a floured surface. Roll out the dough to about 1/8-inch thickness.
    - Use a heart-shaped cookie cutter (about 3-4 inches in size) to cut out heart shapes from the dough.
    - Place a tablespoon of the filling mixture in the center of half of the heart-shaped dough pieces. Brush the edges of the dough with a bit of water.
    - Place a second heart-shaped piece of dough on top of each filled heart and press the edges together to seal. You can use a fork to crimp the edges and ensure they are sealed tightly.
4. **Bake the Calzones:**
    - Brush the tops of the calzones with the beaten egg for a golden finish.
    - Bake in the preheated oven for 15-20 minutes, or until the calzones are golden brown and the filling is hot and bubbly.
5. **Serve:**
    - Allow the calzones to cool slightly before serving.
    - Serve with marinara or pizza sauce for dipping.

Tips:

- **Filling Variations:** Feel free to experiment with different fillings such as sautéed mushrooms, cooked chicken, or various cheeses.
- **Freezing:** Unbaked calzones can be frozen. Assemble them, then freeze on a baking sheet before transferring to a freezer bag. Bake from frozen, adding a few extra minutes to the cooking time.
- **Dough:** If you're short on time, you can use store-bought pizza dough as a quick alternative.

Mini Heart-Shaped Calzones are a delightful way to enjoy classic calzones with a cute and festive twist. They're perfect for sharing with loved ones and make for a fun and tasty addition to any meal. Enjoy these heart-shaped treats!

BBQ Chicken and Pineapple Wraps

Ingredients:

For the BBQ Chicken:

- 2 cups cooked chicken breast, shredded or diced (grilled, baked, or rotisserie chicken works well)
- 1 cup BBQ sauce (store-bought or homemade)
- 1 tablespoon olive oil (optional, for additional flavor)
- 1 teaspoon smoked paprika (optional, for extra smoky flavor)

For the Wraps:

- 4 large flour tortillas or wraps (whole wheat or spinach tortillas work well too)
- 1 cup fresh pineapple, diced (canned pineapple, drained, can also be used)
- 1/2 cup red bell pepper, thinly sliced
- 1/2 cup thinly sliced red onion
- 1 cup shredded lettuce or baby spinach
- 1/2 cup shredded cheese (cheddar, Monterey Jack, or your favorite cheese)
- Fresh cilantro or parsley, chopped (optional, for garnish)

For Serving:

- Extra BBQ sauce or ranch dressing (optional)
- Lime wedges (optional, for a fresh kick)

Instructions:

1. **Prepare the BBQ Chicken:**
   - In a bowl, toss the shredded or diced chicken with the BBQ sauce until well coated. If using olive oil and smoked paprika, mix them in as well for extra flavor.
   - If the chicken is cold, heat it in a skillet over medium heat until warmed through, or microwave it until hot.
2. **Prepare the Wraps:**
   - Lay out the tortillas on a flat surface.
   - Evenly distribute the shredded lettuce or baby spinach in the center of each tortilla.
   - Add the BBQ chicken on top of the lettuce.
   - Sprinkle diced pineapple, red bell pepper slices, and red onion over the chicken.
   - Sprinkle shredded cheese on top of the other ingredients.
3. **Wrap and Serve:**
   - Fold in the sides of the tortilla, then roll it up tightly from the bottom to the top to enclose the filling. You can also use a toothpick to secure the wraps if needed.
   - Slice each wrap in half diagonally for easier handling.
4. **Garnish and Serve:**

- Garnish with chopped fresh cilantro or parsley if desired.
- Serve with extra BBQ sauce, ranch dressing, or lime wedges on the side.

Tips:

- **Chicken:** For a more intense BBQ flavor, marinate the chicken in BBQ sauce for a few hours before cooking.
- **Pineapple:** To enhance the pineapple flavor, you can lightly grill or sauté the pineapple chunks until caramelized.
- **Wrap Variations:** Feel free to add other ingredients like avocado slices, sliced jalapeños for a bit of heat, or diced tomatoes for added freshness.

BBQ Chicken and Pineapple Wraps offer a delightful combination of sweet and savory flavors, wrapped up in a convenient and portable form. They are perfect for a quick meal or a casual get-together, bringing together the best of barbecue and tropical flavors in every bite. Enjoy!

Sweet Potato and Black Bean Tacos

Ingredients:

For the Tacos:

- 2 medium sweet potatoes, peeled and cut into 1/2-inch cubes
- 1 tablespoon olive oil
- 1 teaspoon ground cumin
- 1 teaspoon smoked paprika
- 1/2 teaspoon chili powder
- 1/2 teaspoon garlic powder
- 1/2 teaspoon onion powder
- Salt and freshly ground black pepper, to taste
- 1 can (15 oz) black beans, drained and rinsed
- 1/2 cup red onion, finely diced
- 1/2 cup fresh cilantro, chopped
- 8 small corn or flour tortillas

For the Avocado Lime Crema:

- 1 ripe avocado
- 1/2 cup sour cream or Greek yogurt
- Juice of 1 lime
- 1 clove garlic, minced
- Salt and freshly ground black pepper, to taste

Toppings:

- 1 cup shredded lettuce or cabbage
- 1/2 cup cherry tomatoes, halved
- 1/4 cup crumbled feta cheese or shredded cheese (optional)
- Lime wedges, for serving

Instructions:

1. **Roast the Sweet Potatoes:**
    - Preheat your oven to 425°F (220°C).
    - On a baking sheet, toss the sweet potato cubes with olive oil, cumin, smoked paprika, chili powder, garlic powder, onion powder, salt, and pepper.
    - Spread the sweet potatoes in an even layer and roast for 20-25 minutes, or until tender and lightly caramelized, stirring halfway through.
2. **Prepare the Black Beans:**
    - While the sweet potatoes are roasting, heat the black beans in a small saucepan over medium heat until warmed through. You can add a bit of cumin or chili powder for extra flavor if desired.

3. **Make the Avocado Lime Crema:**
   - In a blender or food processor, combine the avocado, sour cream or Greek yogurt, lime juice, and minced garlic.
   - Blend until smooth and creamy. Season with salt and pepper to taste. If the crema is too thick, you can thin it out with a little water or additional lime juice.
4. **Warm the Tortillas:**
   - Heat the tortillas in a dry skillet over medium heat for about 30 seconds on each side, or until warm and pliable. You can also warm them in the oven or microwave.
5. **Assemble the Tacos:**
   - Spread a layer of roasted sweet potatoes on each tortilla.
   - Top with black beans, diced red onion, and chopped cilantro.
   - Drizzle with the avocado lime crema.
6. **Add Toppings and Serve:**
   - Add shredded lettuce or cabbage, cherry tomatoes, and crumbled feta cheese or shredded cheese if desired.
   - Serve the tacos with lime wedges on the side for an extra burst of freshness.

Tips:

- **Customization:** Feel free to add other toppings like pickled jalapeños, salsa, or hot sauce for extra flavor.
- **Make-Ahead:** You can roast the sweet potatoes and prepare the crema ahead of time for a quicker assembly.
- **Tortillas:** If using store-bought tortillas, consider toasting them slightly to add a bit of crispiness.

Sweet Potato and Black Bean Tacos offer a delightful mix of textures and flavors, with the creamy avocado lime crema perfectly complementing the sweetness of the roasted sweet potatoes and the earthiness of the black beans. These tacos are not only delicious but also a great way to enjoy a plant-based meal that's both satisfying and full of flavor. Enjoy!

Creamy Mushroom and Spinach Orzo

Ingredients:

- 1 tablespoon olive oil
- 1 small onion, finely chopped
- 3 cloves garlic, minced
- 8 oz (225 g) mushrooms, sliced (such as cremini, button, or shiitake)
- 1 cup vegetable or chicken broth
- 1 cup heavy cream or half-and-half
- 1 cup orzo pasta
- 2 cups fresh spinach, roughly chopped
- 1/2 cup grated Parmesan cheese
- 1 teaspoon dried thyme or Italian seasoning
- Salt and freshly ground black pepper, to taste
- Fresh parsley, chopped (for garnish, optional)

Instructions:

1. **Cook the Orzo:**
    - In a medium saucepan, bring a pot of salted water to a boil. Add the orzo and cook according to package instructions until al dente. Drain and set aside.
2. **Prepare the Mushroom and Spinach Mixture:**
    - In a large skillet, heat the olive oil over medium heat.
    - Add the chopped onion and cook until translucent, about 3-4 minutes.
    - Add the minced garlic and cook for an additional 30 seconds until fragrant.
    - Add the sliced mushrooms and cook until they are browned and tender, about 5-7 minutes.
3. **Make the Creamy Sauce:**
    - Pour in the vegetable or chicken broth and bring to a simmer. Cook for about 2 minutes, allowing the broth to reduce slightly.
    - Reduce the heat to low and stir in the heavy cream or half-and-half. Let it simmer gently for 3-4 minutes, allowing the sauce to thicken.
4. **Combine Ingredients:**
    - Add the cooked orzo to the skillet and stir to coat with the sauce.
    - Add the chopped spinach and cook until wilted, about 2 minutes.
    - Stir in the grated Parmesan cheese and season with dried thyme or Italian seasoning, salt, and freshly ground black pepper to taste.
5. **Serve:**
    - Garnish with chopped fresh parsley if desired.
    - Serve immediately while warm.

Tips:

- **Mushrooms:** You can use a mix of different mushrooms for a more complex flavor, or stick with your favorite variety.
- **Creaminess:** For a lighter version, you can substitute the heavy cream with milk or a combination of milk and Greek yogurt.
- **Add-Ins:** Consider adding cooked chicken, bacon, or sautéed shrimp for additional protein.

Creamy Mushroom and Spinach Orzo is a rich and comforting dish that pairs well with a simple green salad or garlic bread. The creamy sauce envelops the tender orzo and the earthy mushrooms, while the fresh spinach adds a burst of color and nutrition. This dish is perfect for a cozy dinner or a special occasion. Enjoy!

Heart-Shaped Sweetheart Sushi Rolls

Ingredients:

For the Sushi Rice:

- 1 1/2 cups sushi or short-grain rice
- 1 3/4 cups water
- 1/4 cup rice vinegar
- 2 tablespoons sugar
- 1 teaspoon salt

For the Sushi Rolls:

- 4 sheets nori (seaweed)
- 1/2 cucumber, julienned
- 1 avocado, sliced
- 4 oz (115 g) cooked crab meat, shrimp, or smoked salmon
- Soy sauce, for dipping
- Pickled ginger and wasabi, for serving

For the Heart-Shaped Cutouts:

- Heart-shaped cookie cutter or sushi mold (if available)
- Fresh chives or green onions, finely chopped (optional, for garnish)

Instructions:

1. **Prepare the Sushi Rice:**
   - Rinse the sushi rice under cold water until the water runs clear to remove excess starch.
   - In a rice cooker or saucepan, combine the rinsed rice and water. Cook according to the rice cooker's instructions or bring to a boil, then reduce heat to low, cover, and simmer for 18-20 minutes. Let it sit covered for 10 minutes after cooking.
   - In a small bowl, mix the rice vinegar, sugar, and salt until dissolved. Gently fold this mixture into the cooked rice while it's still warm. Allow the rice to cool to room temperature.
2. **Prepare the Sushi Rolls:**
   - Place a bamboo sushi mat on a clean surface and lay a sheet of nori, shiny side down, on the mat.
   - Wet your hands to prevent sticking and spread a thin, even layer of sushi rice over the nori, leaving a 1-inch border at the top edge.
   - Lay a few julienned cucumber slices, avocado slices, and your choice of protein (crab meat, shrimp, or smoked salmon) in a horizontal line across the middle of the rice.

- Carefully roll the sushi tightly using the bamboo mat as a guide, pressing gently to ensure a tight roll. Seal the edge with a little water.
3. **Shape the Rolls:**
    - Using a sharp knife, cut the sushi roll into bite-sized pieces. Alternatively, you can use a heart-shaped cookie cutter or sushi mold to cut out heart shapes from the rolls.
    - If using a cookie cutter, press the cutter firmly into the roll to create heart shapes. If you're using a sushi mold, follow the mold's instructions for shaping.
4. **Garnish and Serve:**
    - Arrange the heart-shaped sushi rolls on a serving platter.
    - Garnish with finely chopped chives or green onions if desired.
    - Serve with soy sauce, pickled ginger, and wasabi on the side.

Tips:

- **Rice Preparation:** Be sure to use sushi rice, as it has the right sticky consistency for making rolls. Other types of rice won't work as well.
- **Nori:** Ensure the nori is fresh and crisp for the best flavor and texture.
- **Variations:** Feel free to customize your fillings with other vegetables or seafood according to your preference.
- **Cutting:** Use a sharp knife to cut the rolls and clean the knife between cuts to prevent the rice from sticking.

Heart-Shaped Sweetheart Sushi Rolls are a delightful and creative way to enjoy sushi with a romantic flair. The heart shape adds a special touch, making these rolls perfect for celebrating with loved ones. Enjoy making and sharing these sweet and savory sushi treats!